Cultural Awareness in Teaching Art and Design

I0473466

Cultural Awareness in Teaching Art and Design addresses an emerging area of development in contemporary pedagogy, the fostering of cultural awareness and sensitivity in the designers of tomorrow.

By offering new and unique examples of how to better educate students around issues of cultural awareness, this book presents teaching methodologies that ultimately facilitate students in becoming better, and more inclusive, art and design professionals. Today, the role of education in the addressing of social and cultural issues is increasingly seen as central to pedagogical methodologies. Through engaged teaching, experiential learning, socially orientated pedagogy or any other definition, the idea that students can and should be exposed to, and deal with, issues of importance to various stakeholders is increasingly seen as central to the teaching and learning experience – whether it be in relation to local communities, national economies, regional cultural identities or more. This is explored in a series of innovative, cross-disciplinary case studies in art and design teaching, with authors approaching questions of cultural awareness and engagement through the lenses of art history, product design, communication design, film, architecture and interior design. In presenting their pedagogical methodologies and case studies, the authors in this text offer a unique cross-disciplinary design perspective that captures the cultural and social concerns of several regions of the world: Europe, North America, Asia and Africa and the Middle East.

This book will be an essential reading for art and design educators and students interested in developing and applying models of cultural awareness and engagement in the classroom and studio.

Kirsty Macari is the Co-Head of Undergraduate Programmes in DJCAD at the University of Dundee, which includes Architecture, Urban Planning and Contemporary Art Practice. Kirsty studied Town and Regional Planning and Urban Design combined with significant experience of public and private sector practices across Planning and Economic Development before joining the University of Dundee. She is the Deputy Chair and a Board Member of Architecture & Design Scotland and the Deputy Chair of the Planning Schools Forum. Her research interests are focussed on design thinking within built environment professions and practice-based learning.

Routledge Focus on Design Pedagogy
Series Editor: Graham Cairns

The Routledge Focus on Design Pedagogy series provides the reader with the latest scholarship for instructors who educate designers. The series publishes research from across the globe and covers areas as diverse as beginning design and foundational design, architecture, product design, interior design, fashion design, landscape architecture, urban design, and architectural conservation and historic preservation. By making these studies available to the worldwide academic community, the series aims to promote quality design education.

Fluid Space and Transformational Learning
Kyriaki Tsoukala

Progressive Studio Pedagogy
Examples from Architecture and Allied Design Fields
Edited by Charlie Smith

Emerging Practices in Architectural Pedagogy
Accommodating an Uncertain Future
Edited by Laura Sanderson and Sally Stone

Teaching Architecture(s) in the Post-Covid Era
The New Age of Digital Design
Edited by Sadiyah Geyer

Cultural Awareness in Teaching Art and Design
Edited by Kirsty Macari

For more information about this series, please visit: https://www.routledge.com/architecture/series/RFDP

Cultural Awareness in Teaching Art and Design

**Edited by
Kirsty Macari**

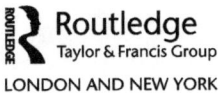 Routledge
Taylor & Francis Group

LONDON AND NEW YORK

First published 2024
by Routledge
4 Park Square, Milton Park, Abingdon, Oxon OX14 4RN

and by Routledge
605 Third Avenue, New York, NY 10158

Routledge is an imprint of the Taylor & Francis Group, an informa business

© 2024 selection and editorial matter, Kirsty Macari; individual chapters, the contributors

British Library Cataloguing-in-Publication Data
A catalogue record for this book is available from the British Library

Library of Congress Cataloging-in-Publication Data
Names: Macari, Kirsty, editor.
Title: Cultural awareness in teaching art and design / edited by Kirsty Macari.
Description: Abingdon, Oxon : Routledge, 2025. | Series: Routledge focus on design pedagogy | Includes bibliographical references and index.
Identifiers: LCCN 2024014349 (print) | LCCN 2024014350 (ebook) | ISBN 9781032616612 (hardback) | ISBN 9781032616629 (paperback) | ISBN 9781032616650 (ebook)
Subjects: LCSH: Art—Study and teaching—Social aspects. | Design—Study and teaching—Social aspects. | Education—Social aspects. | Cultural awareness.
Classification: LCC N85 .C847 2025 (print) | LCC N85 (ebook) | DDC 744.071—dc23/eng/20240425
LC record available at https://lccn.loc.gov/2024014349
LC ebook record available at https://lccn.loc.gov/2024014350

ISBN: 978-1-032-61661-2 (hbk)
ISBN: 978-1-032-61662-9 (pbk)
ISBN: 978-1-032-61665-0 (ebk)

DOI: 10.4324/9781032616650

Typeset in Times New Roman
by codeMantra

Contents

Figures

Contributors

Minjee Jeon is an Assistant Professor in Graphic Design at Montana State University. Her research focusses on the analysis of how media paradigms have evolved in relation to rapid technological advances and their impact on human behaviour. She uses motion-based audiovisual, projection, and participatory work to create biologically inspired speculative designs that aim to build cognitive flexibility. She serves as a coordinator and co-PI for Project MT 988, which creates socially conscious initiatives and promotes art and design-driven social change through pedagogy and outreach. Minjee holds a Master's degree in Visual Communication Design from Virginia Commonwealth University and a BFA in Graphic Design from Iowa State University.

Mbali Khoza is a Visual Artist and Art History and Visual Arts Lecturer at Rhodes University interrogating authorial identity in artistic practice by posing the question 'what difference does it make "who" is speaking?'. Khoza has participated in several group and solo exhibitions, including After Tears, New York (2013) and Native of Nowhere, Cape Town. She is a PhD student at Wits School of Arts as a History of Art examining the historicity of blackness, black existence and black expressive culture. Her publications include *Seeing Blackness through Black Expressive Culture: A Reading of Zanele Muholi's Somnyama Ngonyama – Hail the Dark Lioness* (2021).

Kirsty Macari is the Co-Head of Undergraduate Programmes in DJCAD at the University of Dundee which includes Architecture, Urban Planning and Contemporary Art Practice. Kirsty studied Town and Regional Planning and Urban Design combined with significant experience of public and private sector practices across Planning and Economic Development before joining the University of Dundee. She is the Deputy Chair and a Board Member of Architecture & Design Scotland and the Deputy Chair of the Planning Schools Forum. Her research interests are focussed on design thinking within built environment professions and practice-based learning.

Sarah Mills is an Architect and Head of the Leeds School of Architecture at Leeds Beckett University. Educated at the Architectural Association and The Bartlett, London, she co-directed the MArch studio 'Cinematic Commons' with Dr. Doreen Bernath from 2013 to 2022. Sarah's research reconsiders future models of interdisciplinary practice and the relationship between architecture and film in challenging urban conditions.

Lisa Phillips, NCIDQ, is an Associate Professor of Interior Design at Thomas Jefferson University in Philadelphia. She has a Bachelor of Architecture degree and Master of Education degree, both from Temple University. Ms. Phillips has over 20 years of experience teaching in interior design and has won numerous teaching awards, including Design Intelligence's 25 Most Admired Educators for 2017–2018. She teaches design studios, visualization courses, and capstone research and programming. Her research includes design andragogy, designing spaces to promote wellness and reduce stress, and the study of materiality as it relates to sensory input and the user experience.

Keni Segal has over 30 years of experience in design and design education. He founded the Department of Industrial Design at Hadassah College and was the Head of Department for over a decade, as well as the Head of Leadership Excellence Program. He was the Founder and Head of the Industrial Design Department at Shenkar School of Engineering and Design, creating the academic program of BDes in Industrial Design. He was the lead designer of light rail in Jerusalem and Tel Aviv and the BRT systems of Haifa and Jerusalem. He is an Associate Professor of Design at Hadassah College and CEO of PublicZone Transportation Design Studio.

Jonathan Ventura (PhD) is a Design Researcher, teaching at the Department of Inclusive Design at Hadassah Academic College, Jerusalem, and the Chair of The Unit for History and Philosophy of Art, Design and Technology at Shenkar: Engineering. Design. Art. Jonathan is a Research Fellow at the Helen Hamlyn Centre for Design, Royal College of Art, London, and a fellow at the PhD School at MOME University in Budapest. He specializes in design theory, design anthropology, and social and medical design. Jonathan is the co-founder and co-director of the international Social Design Network (www.socialdesignnetwork.org). His latest book, titled *Introduction to Design Theory* (2023), was co-authored with Prof. Michelle Gal.

Acknowledgements

With thanks first and foremost to the authors in this book (Minjee Jeon, Mbali Khoza, Sarah Mills, Lisa Phillips, Keni Segal and Jonathan Ventura) not only for the collective challenge and enthusiasm in considering cultural awareness across a variety of art and design programmes but in their patience of navigating this journey.

This opportunity would not have started without the support of colleagues across a number of programmes within Duncan of Jordanstone College of Art and Design (DJCAD), University of Dundee with whom I started engagement at Amps conferences with and whose discussions have guided pathways for collaborative and creative conversations. With particular thanks to Helen O'Connor, Programme Director MArch (Hons) Architecture with Urban Planning and the many current and previous architecture and urban planning students who have embraced opportunities to engage in new thinking for future practice and the power of design in ensuring we drive equitable and sustainable places.

Finally, to my husband, Paul and children Katie and Zach, this book is dedicated to you for having patience and support throughout and giving me encouragement and time to allow this book to be completed. You very much recognised the long days and late nights added to daily family life.

1 Introduction

Cultural Relevance and Empathy through Experiential Learning

Kirsty Macari

This chapter contextualises the case studies related to engaged teaching and learning with communities and that are encouraging cultural awareness. It considers the need for empathy and reflection from educators and students. This book is an exploration of the experiences that educators, students, and collaborators have been on through a variety of art and design subject lenses in embedding cultural competencies in education.

Through art and design education and the creative industries, we can explore, reflect on, and design for social justice only when we understand the impact of embedding cultural awareness in our thinking and making.

By offering a position in relation to experiential learning within cultural contexts, we explore some of the challenges that arise and highlight where education allows us to embrace empathy within our fields. This chapter provides a brief overview of each case study, in turn, and the specific knowledge contributions with key themes in the literature and practice experienced along with the conceptual ideas within art and design disciplines.

Experiential learning, clearly framed within the work of John Dewey and further developed by David Kolb,[1] has influenced and encouraged an effective approach to education that not only creates opportunities for learners to engage in direct experiences but also that of reflection. As our places of living, learning, and work continue to evolve, this approach to experiential learning is significant in aiding understanding of different perspectives within multicultural and diverse contexts. The role of empathy within this is essential in allowing for understanding beyond our own bias.

Experiential Learning and Empathy

Empathy within cultural contexts enables learners to connect between their own perspectives and of others, recognising gaps, or indeed unknown connections that can help to embrace understanding within and through cultural experiences. Empathy consists of cognitive, emotive, and behavioural dimensions and is often explored readily within medical education.[2,3] However, medical and design professionals alike must empathise on a day-to-day basis,

DOI: 10.4324/9781032616650-1

putting themselves in the shoes of others to understand a problem and empathise with the perspective of another. Jeremy Till[4] suggests that the fundamental element of a "socially engaged architect" is empathy and is the act of ensuring that all representative voices related to a project are heard in a way that is respectful of the distinct types of knowledge that people can bring. Till goes on to suggest that an empathetic approach is still limited but that this need is being further demanded by students. Designers must be able to anticipate how different users or clients will engage and react with a design. Is there enough done to teach empathy?

With cognitive empathy, we seek to understand a person's perspective and position along with their beliefs and emotions. Experiential learners should seek to actively understand the cultural background of others, and in doing so create opportunities that allow exploration and understanding of another person's perspective, beliefs, and emotions. In experiential learning, we can begin to understand the norms, values, and cultural background of others. This, in turn, can facilitate improved communication. Binder and Holla[5] suggest that even when not fully successful, the attempt to understand another perspective is positive; however, an inherit risk exists where assumptions can skew what another's reality actually is.

Emotional empathy allows individuals to have realised a shared emotional experience felt by others. A sense of connection between individuals involved in the process or meeting can foster a sense of compassion and genuine sense of support and willingness to learn from one another.

Cultural Relevance within Experiential Learning

The ability to undertake "learning by doing" is often the way that experiential learning is positioned. This encourages learners, regardless of subject area, to participate and engage with and within the places around them and beyond.

Within places of diverse societies, experiential learning can encourage and facilitate cultural understanding, by increasing awareness and appreciation of perspectives and traditions beyond a familiar culture of our own.

The ability to work within key components of experiential learning enhances our understanding through the concrete experiences, reflective observations, abstract conceptualisation, and active experimentation as set out by Dewey and Kolb, respectively.

When someone can immerse themself into different cultural contexts, participate in conversations and experiences with people from a variety of diverse backgrounds which allows for all participants, not just the student or educator to gain firsthand experience.

Experiential learning as a process can encourage a cultural competency, an ability to communicate and engage with others. Out with art and design practice, we see this phrase used regularly within the areas of health, medicine, and psychology with regular mention of cultural competency training and cultural competence within the profession (Dana and Allen[6]; So and Rodrigues[7]; Nair and Adetayo[8]). Regardless of profession, they each seek to communicate and engage effectively with others. This can be fostered through the awareness of others and their cultural position, often immersed within a place outside the classroom and encouraging a sharing of dialogue between the community and the students. It can encourage students to apply the direct experience through the project alongside existing curriculum content. Furthermore, it allows for reflection on the experiences by both students and academics, considering challenges and opportunities that have arisen during that time as expressed by Gainsford and Robertson.[9] A necessary experience to ensure any individual also understands their own cultural biases as well as that of those they engage with or in the future may represent within practice.

To build and have empathy within diverse cultural experiences requires individuals to be able to understand, recognise, and accept the validity of others' thoughts, positions, and experiences. Experiential learning can create space to build cultural empathy with others through exposure to people through learning, addressing issues of stereotypes, misunderstanding, and simple unknown knowledge. It can create opportunities to nurture connections between individuals from diverse cultures. Findelli[10] suggests the need for ethical education within the subject of design to ensure designers are conscious of the impact of their own position in making design decisions.

We see attempts to mitigate this risk and embrace ethical education through various disciplines. Architecture education is one such example through a group of students and alumni who, in 2020, created Decolonise Architecture.[11] This opened a dialogue within architecture education that considered institutional bias and systemic racism.

Challenges in Embracing Empathy

Experiential learning, whilst a positive way to embrace learning with and from others, also brings challenges. Considering unconscious bias and stereotyping where learners and educators alike risk bringing unconscious biases and stereotype positions into experiential learning. Recognising and addressing when this occurs are essential and require ongoing training and reminding in relation to one's own position. Is this exacerbated by the homogenous nature of the student population where, even with ambitions to widen access, we still see limited ethnic and socio-cultural diversity? How do we ensure that students can relate to the life experiences of others and minimise unintended consequences of issues such as cultural appropriation.

The cultural appropriation intended or otherwise, through the adoption of any aspect of a culture without full understanding or respecting of it and what this may mean, can have an impact not only within the learning environment but beyond into practice. Avoidance of this situation requires learners to respect boundaries. The potential harm that this can cause is discussed further by Lalonde[12] outlining nonrecognition, misrecognition, and exploitation which can result in invisibility and stereotyping of different cultures.

Experiential learning can result in ethical dilemmas and in particular because of personal values conflict between the learner and the experience. This requires balanced considerations to be made by the learner and therein the consideration of the role of the university to ensure that students understand social responsibility[13] and have civic awareness.[14]

Finally, power imbalances, with a dominant culture by the learner in comparison to that of others, can, through unintentional influence, impact on the wider experiential learning and opportunity to embrace this with empathy. The influences and inequalities that can occur in relation to hierarchy or culture may unintentionally reinforce that which already exists or exacerbate them. Learners must ensure that they acknowledge these influences when considering their approach and influence on engagement with others.

Strategies for Overcoming Challenges and Promoting Empathy

Adopting strategies, both as educators and as learners, to overcome challenges within experiential learning and to enhance a sense of empathy, is essential to ensure success.

The Decolonise Architecture Alternative Reading List[15] is an open access list of articles, journals, podcasts, reports, videos, and books which are built from a compilation of suggestions from anyone who wishes to contribute. However going beyond an alternative reading list to ensure that the discipline can discuss social issues within the Design Studio is necessary. Widening the precedents of global architecture to inform history, theory and humanities education and is recognised within the professional body accreditation of the Architects Registration Board (ARB)[16] and Royal Institute of British Architects (RIBA).[17] This ensures the accurate representation of historic and political contexts are visible within teaching and assessments and supported by diversity workshops to tackle subconscious bias and prejudice.

Within art and design education, other approaches are also adopted such as creative body-based learning (CBL)[18] as a meaningful way to encourage effective strategies for students to consider their own dominant culture conditioning and see this through art and design practices. In this way, through sensory experiences, students can use the practice of art and design to engage with complex issues of oppression. Like the afore-mentioned Decolonise Architecture, this approach could also be considered as having the potential to create informed communities of practice (COP).[19]

It also requires planned and participatory facilitated reflection to ensure that the experiences and emotions are processed as well as address challenges faced by educators and learners. The ability to explore issues and engage in discussion can ensure that individuals can understand their own cultural biases and provide empathy towards those of others. Beyond this, a learner must be engaged with critical reflection of themself, reflecting on their own biases and perspectives. Methods for this should be embedded throughout experiential learning and undertaken through discussions with others, personal journalling, vlogs, or other appropriate means that create space for a regular reflective process.

Ethical guidelines or a framework are necessary if we consider the challenges that can be faced when addressing culture for educators and learners. Educational theorist, Zembylas,[20] refers to "a pedagogy of discomfort" when addressing issues in higher education as outlined by MacGill.[21] Prior to participating in experiential learning experiences, learners must be prepared for and act upon any ethical dilemmas which may require them to make culturally sensitive decisions.

Examples of Art and Design-Based Experiential Learning

Art-based learning and research as explored by Leavy[22] can be both evocative and provocative with the ability for the arts to be "emotionally and politically evocative, captivating, aesthetically powerful and moving." The chapters in this book explore different perspectives of experiential learning through a variety of art and design subjects. Each chapter is shaped through perspectives of the author as an educator or that of their students over a variety of time periods.

Chapter 2 considers the need for correct storytelling to change and challenge discourse in relation to black art histories and multi-modal black expressive cultures. It encourages the need to question existing curriculum and in doing so, through new conversations about black art practitioners, transform approaches to the curriculum. The chapter author reflects on their own experience as an undergraduate art history and visual culture student and the continued call for decolonising of the curriculum.[23] They suggest that differences are important, across the various ethnicities, genders, classes, and geographies which are relevant in framing the identity of blackness and in doing so recognising that both art practitioners and educators to re-learn. Therefore, ensuring that the untold stories become the correct stories of identity in which experiential learners and the communities that they learn in can thrive.

In Chapter 3, the experience of several years of teaching has allowed for an evolved pedagogical strategy to be developed based on two theoretical prisms – the cultural object and design empathy. A focus on values to establish goals, perceptions, and practices within experiential learning allows for an understanding of design culture and thus "value-orientated design" ensuring from the very beginning that the design brief reflects moral and ethical values. The approach reinforces the necessity of self-reflection to be built within the pedagogical approach and ensure that students can use this to question their perspectives, not only of their own culture but of what they are experiencing. Rather than position themselves to design for a culture, they use the engagement and exploration of the culture to question themselves and the issues they experience. It highlights the need to embed empathy within much more design orientated subjects than those normally associated with empathetic design such as healthcare, medical, or inclusive design.

The project Sensory Type in Chapter 4 is framed by the embedding of diversity, equity, and inclusion. It suggests that students can be equipped with a flexible and open mindset and that by embracing diverse and innovative audio-visual communications can be encouraged and prepared to tackle issues in areas of socio-cultural and technology through immersive experiences. Audio-visual communication design can foster ethical, humanistic, and sustainable dialogues within the education context and beyond into the design practices of the future.

Questioning modernity and that of traditional practices in Japan is explored in Chapter 5. The role of community within design and expressed within the medium of film to create new knowledge through collaboration encourages discussion rather than dissemination about a place. Even within the subject of architecture evidenced in this chapter through the experiential architectural education, film was found to be a means to engage with the community and create linkages between the community of a place and visitors.

Chapter 6 explores the symbiotic relationship between commerce and community with interior design students investigating hypothetical projects related to clearly established issues faced today in business through changing behaviours and attitudes to consumerism. The ability to respond to a place identity which, in turn, is shown through branding and products encourages learners to think beyond their own preferences and biases.

The concluding chapter draws together thinking about the future of experiential learning because of those outlined within the rest of the book. It seeks to draw on the cultural contexts and unique opportunities that are created through experiential learning that can encourage empathy and to promote opportunities that embed cultural competencies within learners and the curriculum. The book highlights the need for positive and proactive strategies when considering experiential learning to allow for the challenges that can occur such as cultural bias, ethical dilemmas, and power positions to be addressed before, during, and after the experience. There is a need for constant reflection for both educators and learners alike and a recognition of the challenges that are faced in dealing with multicultural contexts.

Notes

1 David Kolb, *Experiential Learning: Experience as the Source of Learning and Development* (Hoboken, NJ: Prentice-Hall, 1984).

2 Kathy A. Stepien and Amy Baernstein, "Educating for Empathy," *Journal of General Internal Medicine* 21 (2006): 524–530.
3 Peter Irving and David Dickson, "Empathy: Towards a Conceptual Framework for Health Professionals," *International Journal of Health Care Quality Assurance* 17, no. 4 (2004): 212–220.
4 Jeremy Till, Foreword to *The Routledge Companion to Architecture and Social Engagement* (Abingdon: Routledge, 2018).
5 Nadine Binder and Jana Hollá, "Can You Fit a Square into a Circle? Leveraging Experiential Learning to Enhance Relational Capacity Building," in *A Relational View on Cultural Complexity, Relational Economics and Organization Governance*, ed. Baumann Montecinos et al. (Cham: Springer, 2023).
6 Richard Dana and Allen James (Eds.), *Cultural Competency Training in a Global Society* (New York, NY: Springer New York, 2008).
7 Neda So and Michelle Rodrigues, "Cultural Competency," in *Cultural Practices and Dermatoses*, ed. N. A. Vashi (Cham: Springer, 2021).
8 Lakshmi Nair and Adetayo Oluwaseun, "Cultural Competence and Ethnic Diversity in Healthcare," *Plastic and Reconstructive Surgery. Global Open* 7, no. 5 (2019): 2219.
9 Annette Gainsford and Su Robertson, "Yarning Shares Knowledge: Wiradyuri Storytelling, Cultural Immersion and Video Reflection," *The Law Teacher* 53, no. 4 (2019): 500–512.
10 Alain Findeli, "Rethinking Design Education for the 21st Century: Theoretical, Methodological, and Ethical Discussion," *Design Issues* 17, no. 1 (2001): 5–17.
11 Decolonise Architecture, "Decolonise Architecture," accessed December 1, 2023, https://www.decolonisearchitecture.com/.
12 Dianne Lalonde, "Does Cultural Appropriation Cause Harm?" *Politics, Groups, and Identities* 9, no. 2 (2021): 329–346.
13 Susan D. Steiner and Mary A. Watson, "The Service-Learning Component in Business Education: The Values Linkage Void," *Academy of Management Learning & Education* 5, no. 4 (2006): 422–434.
14 Lorraine McIlrath (Ed.) and Iain Mac Labhrainn, *Higher Education and Civic Engagement: International Perspectives* (Hampshire: Ashgate Publishing, Ltd., 2007).
15 Decolonise Architecture, "Decolonise Architecture Alternative Reading List," accessed December 1, 2023, https://www.decolonisearchitecture.com/alternative-reading-list.
16 Architects Registration Board, "About Us," accessed December 10, 2023, https://arb.org.uk/about-arb/.
17 Royal Institute of British Architects, "About RIBA," accessed December 12, 2023, https://www.architecture.com/explore-architecture.
18 Belinda MacGill, "Decolonising Art and Design Education through Standpoint Theory, Embodied Learning and Deep Listening," *The International Journal of Art & Design* 42, no. 4 (2023): 509–520.
19 Jean Lave and Wenger Etienne, *Situated Learning: Legitimate Peripheral Participation* (Cambridge: Cambridge University Press, 1991).
20 Michalinos Zembylas, "'Pedagogy of Discomfort' and Its Ethical Implications: The Tensions of Ethical Violence in Social Justice Education," *Ethics and Education* 10, no. 2 (2015): 163–174.
21 MacGill, "Decolonising Art and Design Education through Standpoint Theory, Embodied Learning and Deep Listening," 509–520.
22 Patricia Leavey, *Method Meets Art*. 3rd ed. (New York: The Guildford Press, 2020), 24.
23 Malose Langa, "Researching the #FeesMustFall Movement," in *#Hashtag: An Analysis of the #FeesMustFall Movement at South African Universities*, ed. Malose Langa (Johannesburg: Centre for the Study of Violence and Reconciliation, 2017).

References

Architects Registration Board. "About Us." Accessed December 10, 2023. https://arb. org.uk/about-arb/.

Baumann Montecinos, J., T. Grünfelder and J. Wieland. *A Relational View on Cultural Complexity: Implications for Theory and Practice*. 1st ed. Cham: Springer International Publishing AG, 2023.

Binder, Nadine and Hollá Jana. "Can You Fit a Square into a Circle? Leveraging Experiential Learning to Enhance Relational Capacity Building." In *A Relational View on Cultural Complexity, Relational Economics and Organization Governance*, edited by Baumann Montecinos et al., 243–266. Cham: Springer, 2023. https://doi.org/10.1007/978-3-031-27454-1_13.

Dana, Richard H. and James Allen (Eds.). *Cultural Competency Training in a Global Society*. 1st ed. New York, NY: Springer New York, 2008.

Decolonise Architecture. "Decolonise Architecture." Accessed December 1, 2023. https://www.decolonisearchitecture.com/.

Decolonise Architecture. "Decolonise Architecture Alternative Reading List." Accessed December 1, 2023. https://www.decolonisearchitecture.com/alternative-reading-list.

Findeli, Alain. "Rethinking Design Education for the 21st Century: Theoretical, Methodological, and Ethical Discussion." *Design Issues* 17, no. 1 (2001): 5–17. http://www.jstor.org/stable/1511905.

Gainsford, Annette and Su Robertson. "Yarning Shares Knowledge: Wiradyuri Storytelling, Cultural Immersion and Video Reflection." *The Law Teacher* 53, no. 4 (2019): 500–512. https://doi.org/10.1080/03069400.2019.1667088.

Irving, Peter and David Dickson. "Empathy: Towards a Conceptual Framework for Health Professionals." *International Journal of Health Care Quality Assurance* 17, no. 4 (2004): 212–220. https://doi.org/10.1108/09526860410541531.

Kolb, David A. *Experiential Learning: Experience as the Source of Learning and Development*. Hoboken, NJ: Prentice-Hall, 1984.

Lalonde, Dianne. "Does Cultural Appropriation Cause Harm?" *Politics, Groups, and Identities* 9, no. 2 (2021): 329–346. https://doi.org/10.1080/21565503.2019.1674160.

Langa, Malose. "Researching the #FeesMustFall Movement." In *#Hashtag: An Analysis of the #FeesMustFall Movement at South African Universities*, edited by Malose Langa, 6–12. Johannesburg: Centre for the Study of Violence and Reconciliation, 2017.

Lave, Jean and Etienne Wenger. *Situated Learning: Legitimate Peripheral Participation*. Cambridge: Cambridge University Press, 1991.

Leavey, Patricia. *Method Meets Art*. 3rd ed. New York: The Guilford Press, 2020.

MacGill, Belinda. "Decolonising Art and Design Education through Standpoint Theory, Embodied Learning and Deep Listening." *The International Journal of Art & Design* 42, no. 4 (2023): 509–520. https://doi.org/10.1111/jade.12479.

McIlrath, Lorraine (Ed.), and Iain Mac Labhrainn. *Higher Education and Civic Engagement: International Perspectives*. Hampshire: Ashgate Publishing, Ltd., 2007.

Nair, Lakshmi and Oluwaseun A. Adetayo. "Cultural Competence and Ethnic Diversity in Healthcare." *Plastic and Reconstructive Surgery. Global Open* 7, no. 5 (2019): e2219–e2219. Available at: https://doi.org/10.1097/GOX.0000000000002219.

Royal Institute of British Architects. "About RIBA." Accessed December 12, 2023. https://www.architecture.com/explore-architecture.

So, Neda and Rodrigues, Michelle. "Cultural Competency." In *Cultural Practices and Dermatoses*, edited by N. A. Vashi, 115–134. Cham: Springer, 2021. https://doi.org/10.1007/978-3-030-68992-6_6.

Steiner, Susan D. and Mary A. Watson. "The Service-Learning Component in Business Education: The Values Linkage Void." *Academy of Management Learning & Education* 5, no. 4 (2006): 422–434.

Stepien, Kathleen A. and Amy Baernstein. "Educating for Empathy." *Journal of General Internal Medicine* 21 (2006): 524–530. https://doi.org/10.1111/j.1525-1497.2006.00443.

Till, Jeremy. Foreword to *The Routledge Companion to Architecture and Social Engagement*. Abingdon: Routledge, 2018.

Zembylas, Michalinos. "'Pedagogy of Discomfort' and Its Ethical Implications: The Tensions of Ethical Violence in Social Justice Education." *Ethics and Education* 10, no. 2 (2015): 163–174.

2 Multi-Modes of Erasure

An Analysis of the Art History and Visual Culture Curriculum

Mbali Khoza

Introduction

It is important to make visible the erasure of multi-modal black art histories from the contemporary art history and visual culture curriculum. By "erasure," I mean the many mechanisms that have and can be employed by art educators to delete and omit black visual culture from the contemporary South African art history curriculums. This chapter will show how the inclusion of these untold multi-modal black art histories can spark new conversations about black art practitioners, their work, and the way they choose to express themselves and visualize black life through the use of visual apparatuses. These are stories, this chapter seeks to argue, that can be told through curriculum transformation. To help bolster this hypothesis is research material from my own lived experience as art history student as well as that of other students in South African universities. I have deliberately chosen to include this information because it is rooted in everyday life of students who have to face many challenges[1] when they enter university spaces. This will be followed by a brief outline of relevant scholarly work that has and is being done to motivate institutions of learning and instructors to reconceptualize curriculums, especially their interpersonal relationships with students. As a focus of art history and visual culture as a discipline, its past, present, and future, visual case studies will be scrutinized to evidence what multi-modal black artistic practice looks like; and why they can play a transformative role in what deem to be black artistic as a whole. A formal analysis of two South African art Lerato Shadi's *Seriti Se* and Brazilian artist Paulo Nazareth's series *Cadernos de Africa (Africa Notebook)* will be conducted. The controversial exhibition *Echoing Voices from Within* intended to commemorate the Rhodes Must Fall (RMF) movement will usher in the problem of archaic Western-centric art historical curricula.

My interest in curriculum transformation is informed by two important events: my exposure as an undergraduate art history and visual culture student to a curriculum that centered and valorized Western art history; and the demand by the student-led Fallist movement for "the decolonization of the educational system, transformation of universities to address racial and gender

DOI: 10.4324/9781032616650-2

inequalities in terms of staff composition."[2] Although the student demands were valid, on-going debates about curriculum decolonization have shown that institutional transformation cannot be accomplished simply by employing black academics nor should it be the sole responsibility of black academics to do the work of transformation. In her essay "Trying to Transform," feminist scholar Sara Ahmed argues that for true institutional transformation to take place, institutions must first acknowledge that appointing someone to transform the institution is "not the same thing as an institution being willing to be transformed (by someone who is appointed)."[3] Equally, the inclusion of black scholarship in the curriculum may be one way to help undo Western scholarship's authority over disciplines, but it is not enough. If institutions want to effectively respond to student demands, Ahmed posits, then they need to start "thinking differently." An integral part of this decolonization process requires institutions to acknowledge their complicity: that they are not exterior to but part of the problem that is "under investigation."[4]

To think differently, art historian and curator Nontobeko Ntombela insists, it is imperative that teaching and learning for both teachers and students are not reliant on theoretical frameworks from elsewhere but is drawn from ones that are "premised on understanding the context within which the African learner and teacher lives and works."[5] For Ntombela, the "problem" is not the curriculum itself—though this is not to say that we should not prioritize its transformation. Rather, the "problem" is the way in which the revised curriculum is taught. Unlearning archaic teaching methodologies involves doing what Ahmed describes as "diversity work."[6] This work is an "action,"[7] and such an action or such actions can be multi-modal. For instance, doing diversity work within universities might require scholars to re-evaluate the lenses through which the curriculum is taught. Does it still employ Western ways of seeing? (What are these?) Does it assume an Africentric way of seeing? (What are they?) If so, what does seeing through an Africentric lens mean or look like? Or can we think of non-Western scholarship as scholarship that is in conversation with Western scholarship? I believe we can only answer these questions by reflecting on our approach to teaching and learning. For psychologist Augustine Nwoye, one way that African scholars can ensure that their approach to teaching and learning is "doing diversity work" is by moving away from a "dualistic" interpretation of African society, from an "either-or" approach that posits Eurocentric versus Afrocentric scholarship, to a "both-and" position that provides a much more holistic representation of African society through visual culture.[8]

Ahmed believes that teaching and learning can be diversified by developing new "communication strategies"[9]—in other words, thinking critically about how we design, develop, and deliver our courses. For example, in *Pedagogy of the Oppressed*, Paulo Freire suggests that we rethink "teacher-student relationships" by getting rid of one-directional teaching and learning methodologies that involve a "narrating subject (the teacher) and patient, listening objects (the students)."[10] This can be done by inviting students to contribute to their own learning experience. Ntombela believes that this information can be drawn from their "local contexts and references which may include students' lived experiences."[11] This "learning-centered approach" intends not only to initiate meaningful dialogue between students and teachers but also between peers.[12] These exchanges can be beneficial to the student learning experience in two ways: to identify knowledge gaps students might have and/or to fill them.

So how can the above teaching and learning methodologies be utilized to transform the art history and visual history curriculum? From an art history and visual culture context, "thinking differently" about black art history entails, first, highlighting the contribution of black art practitioners to the discipline by historicizing it. Second, it means asking new questions about black artistic practice, such as, "How can black creativity become critical of itself?"[13] Third, it necessitates ensuring that analysis of black creative production should not be limited to its ability to produce what Michele Wallace describes as "negative/positive images" of blackness, but should allow for "various perspectives."[14] Finally, art historians must be willing to change old narratives about the function of black visual culture, by rejecting claims that black art practitioners' interests are only concerned with black social or political issues. Instead, they should investigate what other, wider interests' black art practitioners may have and engage with these.

Visual Case Studies

To illustrate how this can be achieved, I examine two visual case studies of black artists, whose work I believe are examples of the ways in which black expressive culture is multi-modal. The artists I chose are South African Lerato Shadi and Brazilian Paulo Nazareth. The way they represent blackness differs not only by medium (photography, drawing, sound, text, performance art) but also by the generational time and space in which they produce, reference, or set their work. I am interested in the generational effect of blackness and its production of diverse attitudes of blackness[15]; and in how black South African visual culture is in dialogue with, or at least engaging in the same dialogues as, black people art practitioners living in the diaspora.

The common denominator in Shadi's and Nazareth's works is their use of black subjects and their bodies. This, however, cannot sufficiently represent the complexity of black identity, as I will show. What can visual representations of blackness beyond the body look like? What cultural and historic signifiers, visual language, or apparatuses and vernaculars are deployed by these creative practitioners to signal blackness? What do these visual images tell us about black existence in each spacetime?

"Seriti Se"—an ambiguous Setswana term that speaks to "this dignity, this honor, this aura and this shadow"[16]—is the name Lerato Shadi gave to one of her installations. For her, the process of translation that is required reveals that "translation, in this case, is difficult because it does not take into account the cultural context of what is being translated."[17] The title teaches that translation is based on selection and subjectivity; readers and viewers can interpret it in multiple ways. This inability to fix the title's meaning plays a crucial role in how the work is interpreted by Setswana speakers in contrast to those not fluent in the language.

Written on a white gallery wall with black paint, the names of Black women and women of Color form the starting point of *Seriti Se* (see Figures 2.1 and 2.2). Many of the names belong to historical figures who experienced some form of erasure, in written histories and in digital forms, an erasure that "disappears together with the evidence of its existence."[18] It shows, writes Olu Oguibe, how erasure is "an act without a trace."[19] Viewers are then invited to participate in a performance work to re-create or illustrate what Shadi describes as the "violence of historic erasure" enacted on black women and brown women by Western history, which has become World history. They are provided with a paintbrush and white paint and given the opportunity either to become complicit in the mark of deletion (or at least think about how they are) or do some independent research on the women and their contribution to world history (see Figure 2.2). Central to this body of work is the notion of being seen, particularly the aspect of what the artist wants the viewer to see, or what she wants to show through the use of visual and textual languages (the decision to deliberately title the work in Setswana and not in English,

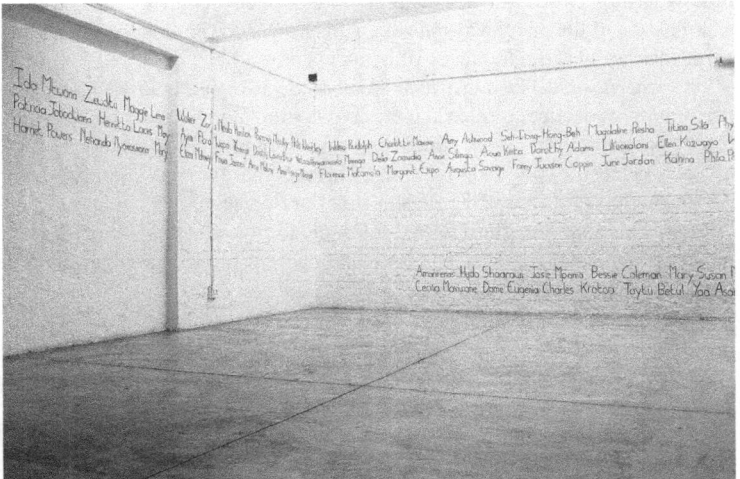

Figure 2.1 Lerato Shadi, Seriti Se, Wall Performance-Drawing Instillation, GoetheOn-Main, Johannesburg (2016).

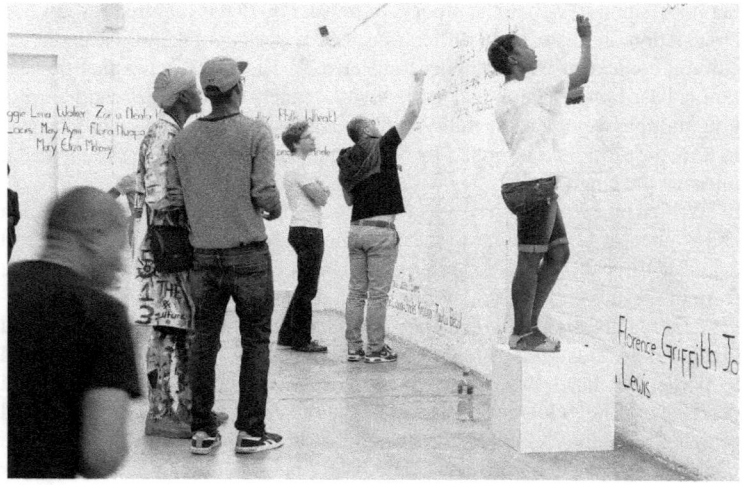

Figure 2.2 Lerato Shadi, Seriti Se, Wall Performance-Drawing Instillation, GoetheOn-Main, Johannesburg (2016).

"the language of the gallery"). Central is drawing attention to how language can be both a tool of inclusivity and, critically, exclusivity. Shadi's interest in how anti-black institutions manifest in this binary is then extended to an examination of the many ways in which this has led to the erasure of the black vernacular, of black individuals, of black histories.

In *Cadernos de Africa* (African Notebooks, 2013–), Paulo Nazareth uses performative practice to trace slavery by walking along former slave routes, from Johannesburg to Lyon. He documents his journey through photographic images, videos, a collection of found objects, and diarized narratives from his encounter with locals. These souvenirs are presented as evidence of his journey. This simple gesture invites the audience to reflect on slavery's transformation of black ethnicity and on contemporary black reconfigurations of blackness—particularly how blackness post-slavery has created new fractions within black communities. For example, the term "African-American" historically represented "two feuding ancestries conjoined by a hyphen," as Jelani Cobbs explains.[20] In North America, blacks have come to know Africa as the first form of difference, Achille Mbembe notes, apart from whiteness.[21] Africa became a symbol of ancestral origin, but an ancestry that could not be traced—a reminder of the brutal history that intervened between Africa and America.[22] Mbembe compares black Americans' encounters with black Africans as an encounter with another's other"[23]; whereas Charles I. Nero

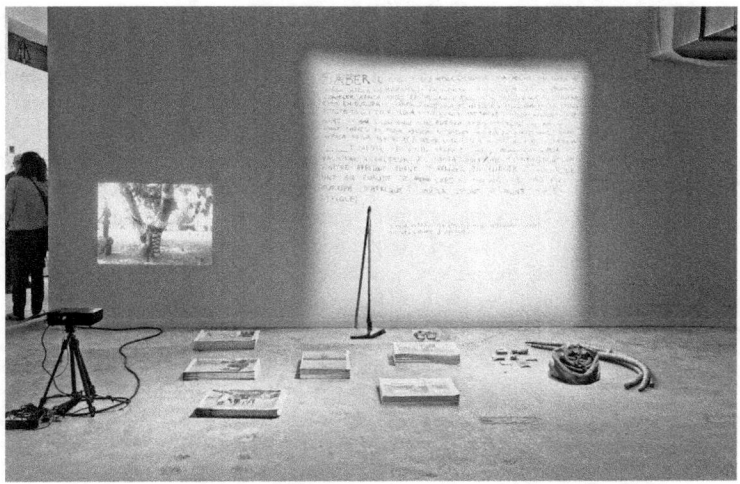

Figure 2.3 Paulo Nazareth, Cadernos de Africa (Africa Notebooks), 2013–, mixed media, dimensions variable, installation view, Institute of Contemporary Art, London.

characterizes Africans from the geographical areas of the historic transatlantic trade but who are not descendants of transatlantic slavery as "differently black" (Figure 2.3).[24]

Nero identifies blacks who are "differently black" as African immigrants living in the United States who, unlike the native-born blacks, do not have a shared history of slavery. This inability to relate to the African-American experience has resulted in ethnic tensions between the black communities, largely because "African immigrants are questioning their racial categorization as Black, which they see as a metonymic device for the inferior position of African Americans relative to Whites."[25]

Failure to acknowledge this "within-group conflict" perpetuates the long-standing myth that the black lived experience is homogenous and that the African-American experience can be lumped with that of African immigrants. To undo these myths, we must recognize that there are, in fact, "differences in ethnicity, nationalism, language, adaptation to life in the United States" among black lives in America and that these differences affect each ethnic group's socio-economic standing with wider society as well as their encounter with White America.[26]

On the 9th of March 2016, exactly a year after the RMF movement began, the Centre of African Studies (CAS) Gallery curated the exhibition titled *Echoing Voices from Within*. The works included in the exhibition consisted of a collection of 75 photographs taken by students who participated in the protest or who were by-standers; memorabilia such as posters and "relevant artefacts that captured the essence and the evolving story of a dramatic year in student protest," as stated on the CAS site.[27] These images and gestures[28] did not make it to the public domain[29] for reasons unknown. Those that did make it online were out of circumstantial reasons: the University of Cape Town's (UCT) Trans Collective. The collectives protest was predicated on all too familiar historical gap on most social justice movement, which have documented as led and originated by cisgender men while erasing, deleting, and omitting the contribution of cisgendered women and the queer community. Addressing the public outside the gallery on the behalf of the collective, HeJin Kim recited the #FeesMustFall slogan, "The revolution will be black-led and intersectional* or it will be bullshit," Kim continued, "This" citing the exhibition is "bullshit."[30] On their Facebook page, they realized a much more extensive public statement, detailing why they believed the exhibition perpetuating the same systemic violence that RMF was trying to dismantle. Titled, *Tokenistic, Objectifying, Voyeuristic Inclusion Is at Least as Disempowering as Complete Exclusion*, it reads:

> Kimberle Crenshaw captures the motivation for the UCT Trans Collective's disruptive intervention at the Rhodes Must Fall movement's one year anniversary exhibition most eloquently.
>
> For the Trans Collective, the commemorations that are happening at this time invite us to reflect on both the decolonial year that has been and the years that are to come. In our reflection we have found that as black, poor, queer, womxn and non-binary trans people our position in the decolonial theory and practice is unchanged.
>
> It was as early as April 2015, just a month after the inception of RMF, that what is now known as the Trans Collective flagged the issue of a rigid loyalty to patriarchy, cisnormativity, heteronormativity and the gender binary within the space. In our founding statement we made it clear that 'we recognize that colonization has had a severe impact on how we perceive gender and gender expression and thus we are reclaiming our space in the globalized decolonization movement and calling for our narrative to be instructive going forward'. However, we had been coerced to construct a smaller decolonial enclave that would run parallel to RMF because of what had become apparent as a gulf in consciousness of many, particularly black cishet men, organizers where the understanding of the colony and how it operates did not connect with an understanding of patriarchy, heteronormativity and gender essentialism as colonially demarcated powers. Often, there was an outright refusal to acknowledge that the condition of being a womxn, queer, trans, disabled and so forth is not incidental to blackness but that these conditions are collateral to blackness. So suffocating is this, that we have had to submarine from active membership. We refuse to avail our bodies and psyches for the violence that has infiltrated

the decolonial project through patriarchy, cisnormativity, heteronormativity and the gender binary. Our role has now evolved into speaking back to RMF and keeping it accountable to its commitment to intersectionality precisely because it is positioned as a black decolonial space. We are black, queer and trans simultaneously. These are not severable, and we deserve to be freed from their colonial baggage simultaneously too.[31]

The above statement exemplifies how "thinking differently" can be actualized. By refusing to put sexuality, gender and class on the backburner, as many cisgender-led movements have argued, the Trans Collective is making it vehemently clear that the notoriety of the Fallist movements was built on the labor of Black and Brown women and the queer community. It is therefore counterrevolutionary to think that these intersecting gender and identity politics should be ignored and are an integral part of the everyday daily lives of non-cisgender communities. I say this with the awareness that in South Africa, femicide, corrective rape, and the murder of queer people within black and brown communities are still an epidemic. Mainly because many of these injustices, even when reported, go unpunished (Figures 2.4 and 2.5).

What the Trans Collective makes visible, and why the decolonial project remains ineffective, especially in the domain of university space where students are sold the illusion that these spaces are democratic, apply free and critical thinking, and are hubs of inclusivity. UCT's failure to reckon with

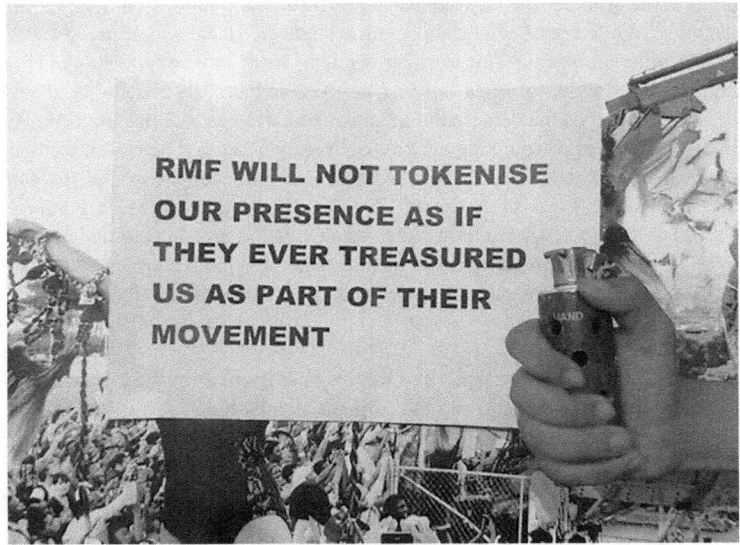

Figure 2.4 A poster shaming the RMF for tokenism. Unknown photographer.

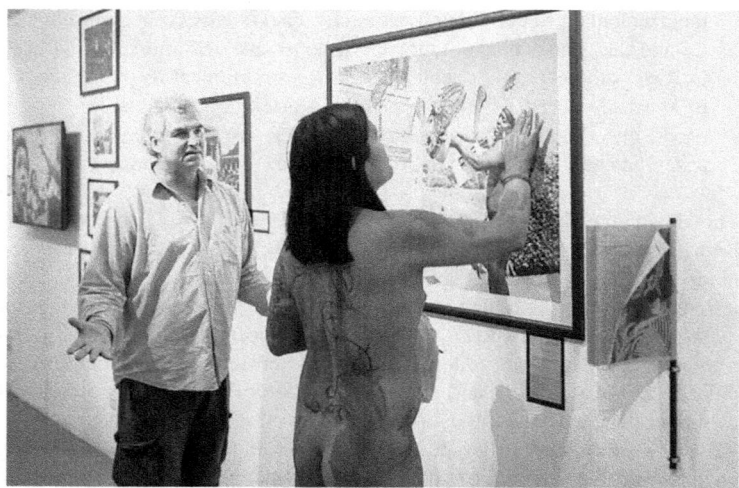

Figure 2.5 Helen Kim, a member of the UCT Trans Collective, writing the word "Rapist" on the infamous photographs of Chumani Maxwele throwing excrement at the Cecil John. Unknown photographer.

its tainted history with Cecil John Rhodes until it was forced too speaks volumes about whether the institutions see its historical relations with Rhodes as damning. While not of equal stature, what binds the statue and *Echoing Voices from Within* is institutions of learning insidious habit of intergenerational erasure. While it might not seem to cause any visible harm, its invisibility attacks the psyche, breeds intergeneration trauma, and leaves its victims fatigued. The Fallist movement, I would argue, were outwardly expressed repressed feelings, predicated on what clinical psychologist Chabani Manganyi terms as the condition of "being-black-in-the-world."[32] Sixteen years later, in 1989, Kimberlé Crenshaw would develop a term "intersectionality" to broaden our understating of Blackness and Brownness as an identity. That it is more than just skin color but a spectrum of being, one that is elevated by sexuality and gender (Figures 2.6 and 2.7).

It is for these reasons, that I find the Trans collectives gestures so compelling, firstly because the use of red paint signals blood, dead, visible violence. In this case, they believed it to be a replica of internalized colonial violence. Secondly their insertion of their bodies into space, speak to the sense of belonging or not belonging in a society is still perceives itself as heteronormativity. What does this mean for our curriculums? Ahmed likens this push for an inclusively of all individuals that of being a "killjoy." She describes it as, feeling like

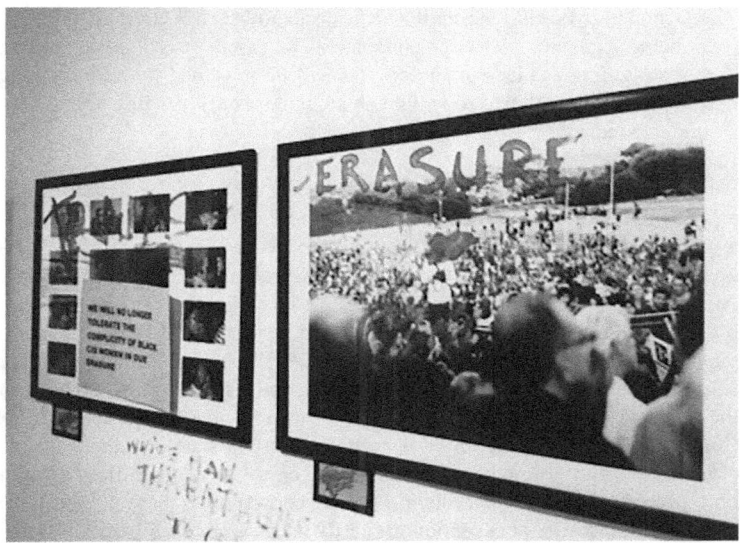

Figure 2.6 The word erasure written on a photography as well as an enactment of the erasure of an individual in the photography. Unknown photographer.

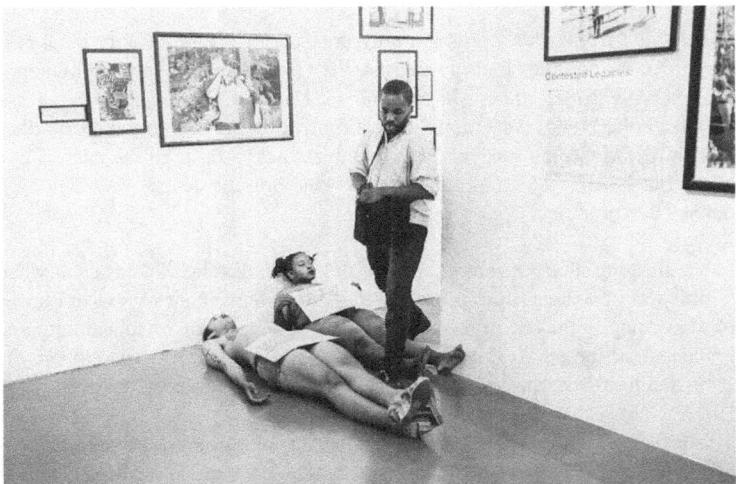

Figure 2.7 Members of the UCT Trans Collective blocked entrances to the exhibition. Photo: Ashraf.

"making your life harder than it is needs to be. ...as if today, just stop noticing exclusive and your burden will be eased. It is implied that by not struggling against something you will be rewarded by an increasing proximity to that thing. You might be included if only you just stop talking about exclusion"[33]

An endeavor she recognized can be ware own done as it is endless. But it is a necessary "feminist survival kit," an ever more effective tool when done as a group as it becomes a form of "feminist self-care."[34] Social justice movements are founded on the philosophy of care. Speaking on the concept of care, Audre Lorde insists that it should not be just mistaken for "self-indulgence" but "self-preservation...that is an act of political warfare."[35] Hence, protests, violent or non-violent, that are invested in the well-being of communities are so passionate. They are rooted in care and empathy for as Lorde explains in the poem, A Litany for Survival, "those of us who live at the shoreline."[36] Consequently, "think differently" is to be in constant state of protest against organization that promote an acceptance of unjust systems inflict on harm on those who have navigate them. Derelict curriculums, that take the form of an exhibition, are no exception primarily because they are in the business of indoctrinating learners into schools of those that can be far removed from their reality or the real world. This is why many students struggle to put any of these theories into practice.

Conclusion

Shadi's and Nazareth's works not only critique European ideas of blackness but mirror the complex multidimensionality of black subjecthood. In his seminal text *Moving the Centre: The Struggle for Cultural Freedom*, Kenyan decolonial scholar Ngũgĩ wa Thiong'o, writing from a literary context, describes this shift from seeing race—in this case blackness—through the perspective of the black self, instead of the West's as "moving the centre." Wa Thiong'o defines this process as

> challenging the Eurocentric basis of the vision of other worlds even when this was of writers who were not necessarily in agreement with what Europe was doing to the rest of the world. It was not a question of substituting one center for the other. The problem arose only when people tried to use the vision from any one center and generalize it as the universal reality.[37]

This process is crucial because it questions anti-black narratives about blackness inherited from the West that still insist that blackness is a collective identity within black communities. This has affected blackness in the following ways: first, it has delayed the process of reconstructing blackness into a multidimensional identity; second, it has made the black self-invisible; and third, it has denied the black self the right to redefine its own identity in relation to blackness.

The danger of these "single stories," as Chimamanda Ngozi Adichie puts,[38] is evident in the inability of art history and visual culture curriculums to acknowledge why its history of erasure—particularly of the many different ways black expressive culture has and continues to grapple with the "everyday life" experience of being black in the world—is a prime example of yet another anti-black institution that mediates who "occupies space, who owns it, who lords over it, and for whose benefit it is worked."[39] Unlearning these racial hierarchies is pertinent if art history and visual culture curriculums want to be truly decolonized. By this, I do not simply mean transforming the curriculum by means of "inclusion," in an attempt to sanitize the violence of exclusionary practices, but the recognition of "the inequalities" of art historical discourses.[40] This is to ensure that art historians do not partake in a false "inclusiveness," one that is similar to "being included in a system that is unjust, violent and unequal."[41] Instead, art historians can create space for black and queer art histories by articulating how these histories have existed visually and textually.

For Mbembe, decolonizing a curriculum "is a project of 're-centering.' It is about rejecting the assumption that the modern West is the central root of Africa's consciousness and cultural heritage. It is about rejecting the notion that Africa is merely an extension of the West."[42]

In so doing, it allows black thinkers and black art practitioners to re-learn what blackness is as a global phenomenon; one that is complicated by what I refer to as "differences that matter," such as ethnicity, gender, class, time, and geography, that must be made visible to avoid reproducing monolithic definitions of blackness.

This is why true circular transformation must involve "critical reflection." Martyn Stewart posits that critical reflection can happen when lecturers create a "safe learning environment" in which students can work through their "existing beliefs, assumptions and attitudes" to "nurture reflective expression."[43] It is in this environment that art historians can begin doing diversity work, which Ahmed defines as "the work we do when we are trying to transform an institution; or, to be more specific, the work we do when are trying to open up institutions to those who have historically been excluded from them."[44] This is the project that was called for by the Fallist movement and, I would argue, that remains unfinished as demonstrated by Trans Collectives protest.

In conclusion, this chapter attempts an articulation of why untold stories about black art histories and multi-modal black expressive cultures, when told correctly, can help change and challenge visual discourses on blackness, particularly racial myths that continue to affect how black expressive culture is constructed, perceived, and consumed. This will, in turn, make art historians re-evaluate their preconceptions about art made by black practitioners and their contribution to art history.

Notes

1 Majority of are the by-product of inescapable political, social, economical factors that have to navigate on a daily bases.
2 Malose Langa, "Researching the #FeesMustFall Movement," in *#Hashtag: An Analysis of the #FeesMustFall Movement at South African Universities*, ed. Malose Langa (Johannesburg: Centre for the Study of Violence and Reconciliation, 2017), 6.
3 Sara Ahmed, *Living a Feminist Life* (Durham, NC: Duke University Press, 2017), 94.
4 Ahmed, *Living*, 94.
5 Nontobeko Ntombela, "Practitioning: A Few Notes on Curatorial Training in Africa," in *ÀSÌKÒ: On the Future of Artistic and Curatorial Pedagogies in Africa*, ed. Bisi Silva et al. (Lagos: Centre for Contemporary Art, 2017), 169.
6 Ahmed, 95.
7 Ahmed, 94.
8 Augustine Nwoye, "An Africentric Theory of Human Personhood," *Psychology in Society* 54 (2017): 43.
9 Ahmed, 95.
10 Paulo Freire, *Pedagogy of the Oppressed* (New York: Continuum, 2005), 71.
11 Ntombela, "Practitioning," 169–170.
12 Ntombela, 169.
13 Michele Wallace, *Invisible Blues: From Pop to Theory* (London: Verso, 2016), 218.
14 Wallace, *Invisible Blues*, 218.
15 Christina M. Greer, *Black Ethnics: Race, Immigration, and the Pursuit of the American Dream* (Oxford: Oxford University Press, 2013), 89.
16 Lerato Shadi, "Violence of Historical Erasure" (Master's thesis, Weißensee Kunsthochschule Berlin, 2018).
17 Shadi, "Violence of Historical Erasure."
18 Olu Oguibe, "Art, Identity, Boundaries: Postmodernism and Contemporary African Art," in *Reading the Contemporary: African Art from Theory to the Market Place*, ed. Olu Oguibe et al. (London: Institution of International Visual Arts, 1999), 17.
19 Oguibe, "Art, Identity, Boundaries," 17.
20 Jelani Cobbs, "Black Panther and the Invention of African," *New Yorker*, February 18, 2018, https://www.newyorker.com/news/daily-comment/black-panther-and-the-invention-of-africa.
21 Achille Mbembe, *Critique of Black Reason* (Johannesburg: Wits University Press, 2017), 25.
22 Cobbs, "Black Panther and the Invention of African."
23 Mbembe, *Critique*, 25.
24 Charles I. Nero, "Differently Black: The Fourth Great Migration and Black Catholic Saints in Ramin Bahrani's *Goodbye Solo* and Jim Sheridan's *In America*," in *Migrating the Black Body: The African Diaspora Visual Culture*, ed. Leigh Raiford et al. (Seattle: University of Washington Press, 2017), 208.
25 Benjamin A. Okonofua, "'I Am Blacker Than You': Theorizing Conflict between African Immigrants and African Americans in the United States," *SAGE Open* 3, 3 (2013): 2.
26 Okonofua, "'I Am Blacker Than You,'" 2.
27 http://www.africanstudies.uct.ac.za/cas/gallery/echoingvoices_rmf
28 A wall with the phrase "Contested Legacies" was curated.
29 They are not available online. One would have to contact CAS to gain access of exhibition images.
30 Y. Omar, "Trans Collective Stops RMF Exhibition," *UCT News*, March 2016, https://www.news.uct.ac.za/article/-2016-03-10-trans-collective-stops-rmf-exhibition.

31 https://www.facebook.com/transuniversityforum/posts/pfbid02dMjhnp1enYdQS
   JU411ttbAMXcBs6LUkBzR5qiLmRTTDtKyNcVCnQE1JBLARsRLHkl,
   accessed February 10, 2023.
32 Chabani Mangani, *Being-Black-in-the-World* (Johannesburg: Raven Press, 1973), 3.
33 Ahmed, 235.
34 Ahmed, 236.
35 Lorde, 131.
36 Ahmed, 236.
37 Ngũgĩ Wa Thiong'o, *Moving the Centre: The Struggle for Cultural Freedom* (London: James Currey, 1993), 22.
38 Chimamanda N. Adichie, "The Danger of a Single Story," TEDGlobal Talk, July 2009, at 0:00 min, https://www.ted.com/talks/chimamanda_ngozi_adichie_the_danger_of_a_single_story?language=en.
39 Okwui Enwezor, "Reframing the Black Subject: Ideology and Fantasy in Contemporary South African Representation," in *Reading the Contemporary: African Art from Theory to the Marketplace*, ed. Olu Oguibe et al. (Cambridge, MA: MIT Press, 1999), 379.
40 Ahmed, 252.
41 Ahmed, 263.
42 Achille Mbembe, "Decolonizing Knowledge and the Question of the Archive," paper presented at the Wits Institute for Social and Economic Research (WISER) (Johannesburg: University of the Witwatersrand, 2015).
43 Martyn Stewart, "Understanding Learning: Theories and Critique," in *University Teaching in Focus: A Learning-Centred Approach*, ed. Lynne Hunt et al. (London: Routledge, 2012), 16.
44 Ahmed, 93.

References

Adichie, Chimamanda N. "The Danger of a Single Story." TEDGlobal Talk, 18:33 min, July 2009. https://www.ted.com/talks/chimamanda_ngozi_adichie_the_danger_of_a_single_story?language=en.

Ahmed, Sara. *Living a Feminist Life*. Durham, NC: Duke University Press, 2017.

Cobbs, Jelani. "Black Panther and the Invention of African." *New Yorker*, February 18, 2018. https://www.newyorker.com/news/daily-comment/black-panther-and-the-invention-of-africa.

Enwezor, Okwui. "Reframing the Black Subject: Ideology and Fantasy in Contemporary South African Representation." In *Reading the Contemporary: African Art from Theory to the Marketplace*, edited by Olu Oguibe and Okwui Enwezor, 377–399. Cambridge, MA: MIT Press, 1999.

Freire, Paulo. *Pedagogy of the Oppressed*. Translated by Myra Ramos. New York: Continuum, 2005.

Greer, Christina M. *Black Ethnics: Race, Immigration, and the Pursuit of the American Dream*. Oxford: Oxford University Press, 2013.

Langa, Malose. "Researching the #FeesMustFall Movement." In *#Hashtag: An Analysis of the #FeesMustFall Movement at South African Universities*, edited by Malose Langa, 6–12. Johannesburg: Centre for the Study of Violence and Reconciliation, 2017.

Lorde, Audrey. *Sister Outside: Essays and Speeches*. Berkley: Cross Press, 1984.

Mbembe, Achille. "Decolonizing Knowledge and the Question of the Archive." Paper presented at the Wits Institute for Social and Economic Research (WISER), University of the Witwatersrand, Johannesburg, 2015.

Mbembe, Achille. *Critique of Black Reason.* Translated by L. Dubois. Johannesburg: Wits University Press, 2017.

Nero, Charles I. "Differently Black: The Fourth Great Migration and Black Catholic Saints in Ramin Bahrani's Goodbye Solo and Jim Sheridan's *In America.*" In *Migrating the Black Body: The African Diaspora Visual Culture,* edited by Leigh Raiford and Heike Raphael-Hernandez, 207–220. Seattle: University of Washington Press, 2017.

Ntombela, Nontobeko. "Practitioning: A Few Notes on Curatorial Training in Africa." In *ÀSÌKÒ: On the Future of Artistic and Curatorial Pedagogies in Africa,* edited by Bisi Silva and Stephanie Baptist, 167–180. Lagos: Centre for Contemporary Art, 2017.

Nwoye, Augustine. "An Africentric Theory of Human Personhood." *Psychology in Society* 54 (2017): 42–66.

Oguibe, Olu. "Art, Identity, Boundaries: Postmodernism and Contemporary African Art." In *Reading the Contemporary: African Art from Theory to the Market Place,* edited by Olu Oguibe and Okwui Enwezor, 17–29. London: Institution of International Visual Arts, 1999.

Okonofua, Benjamin A. "'I Am Blacker Than You': Theorizing Conflict between African Immigrants and African Americans in the United States." *SAGE Open* 3, no. 3 (2013): 1–14.

Shadi, Lerato. "Violence of Historical Erasure." Master's thesis, Weißensee Kunsthochschule Berlin, 2018.

Stewart, Martyn. "Understanding Learning: Theories and Critique." In *University Teaching in Focus: A Learning-Centred Approach,* edited by Lynne Hunt and Denise Chalmers, 3–20. London: Routledge, 2012.

Wa Thiong'o, Ngũgĩ. *Moving the Centre: The Struggle for Cultural Freedom.* London: James Currey, 1993.

Wallace, Michele. *Invisible Blues: From Pop to Theory.* London: Verso, 2016.

3 The Cultural Object, Empathy, and Pedagogy

Keni Segal and Jonathan Ventura

Introduction

"Every people that has produced architecture has evolved its own favourite forms, as peculiar to that people as its language, its dress, or its folklore.
Until the collapse of cultural frontiers in the last century, there were all
over the world distinctive local shapes and details in architecture, and the
buildings of any locality were the beautiful children of a happy marriage
between the imagination of the people and the demands of their countryside. I do not propose to speculate upon the real springs of national
idiosyncrasy, nor could I with any authority. I like to suppose simply that
certain shapes take a people's fancy, and that they make use of them in a
great variety of contexts, perhaps rejecting the unsuitable applications, but
evolving a colourful and emphatic visual language of their own that suits
perfectly their character and their homeland."[1]

In his extremely important architectural project, presented at length in the
book *Architecture for the Poor*, Hassan Fathy laments the Egyptian's tendency
to prefer modernist architecture over local planning and building traditions.
Instead, Fathy worked with local communities in order to better understand
their needs and offer suitable material solutions. In this process, his suggested
tactics proved to be cheaper, more relevant, ecological, and culturally suitable. Unfortunately, influential local and national forces, coupled with petty
politics, influenced his work and brought the whole project to a premature
end. Yet, his poetic account of a lonely International-style white cement building overlooking the Egyptian desert highlights wonderfully the importance
and negligence of vernacular design in favour of famous or desirable styles
of design and building. And indeed, while his work is rightfully considered a
pioneer in vernacular design, it is hardly the only light shining from this piece.
Paving the way for community-led projects, as well as participatory design
and public involvement in architectural projects, all contribute immensely to
contemporary design strategies. Moreover, as a key feature in this chapter,

DOI: 10.4324/9781032616650-3

Fathy calls our attention to two key elements – empathy and the reframing of cultural hierarchies. Indeed, reflecting upon the intricate dialogue between local heritage and the more prestigious colonial visual and material cultural traits stands out in this book, as British and Egyptian traditions fight amidst various professional practices. This ever-present dialogue shares many attributes with the cultural attributes of design in contemporary Israeli society, apart from the common British colonial period.

Indeed, the concept of vernacular design is hardly new. However, while this concept is well-researched in architecture, it is less so in design. As a coherent counterpart, we might consider labelling this approach as 'vernacular design'; yet, we wish to propose an alternative. As this chapter is based on an academic course, we prefer to consider the concept of local design through two complementing theoretical prisms – the cultural object, and design and empathy – which served as key layers in our pedagogic strategies. The common denominator to these concepts is a clearly defined value-oriented basis that establishes goals, perceptions, and practice from the get-go. Conversely, Julier[2] described design culture as consisting of both a broad socio-cultural context and subsequent practical ramifications and ethical boundaries. Furthermore, design culture is not only contextualized but is very much a process, not a quick search for a solution. Following Julier's identification of this approach as agentic, Manzini[3] adds the importance of collective effort, culminating in processes of co-design as an ideological, practical, and theoretical decision. To these important understandings of design culture, we added a layer of what we term 'value-oriented' design, i.e., professing certain moral and ethical values that define the design brief from the first day. In addition, creating empathy for one's intricate local cultural surroundings can be more easily achieved through relating to the seemingly alien intricacies of another's. With these in mind, we obviously did not set out to design for other cultures; rather we aimed at creating a mixture of other rich cultures with contemporary Israeli cultures, serving to trigger questions and wicked problems from our students' own realities. We found this method highly important since it served two purposes: first, we led our students to question their own conventions, after a much-needed self-reflection; second, we opened a window for them to be acquainted with other cultures, thus further promoting the acceptance of other cultures. For these purposes, then, the mega-cultural complex socio-cultural world of African societies offered an almost array of possibilities (after surpassing the seemingly obvious warning to the students that 'there is no Africa, but an almost endless Africas'). Japanese classic culture offered a multi-faceted conflicting and contradicting scenario, much needed in the ultra-dichotomized and uber-binary cultural understanding which has become contemporary Israeli social reality.

Therefore, taking these concepts into account, we developed a studio for fourth-year students at the Department of Inclusive Design at HAC in Jerusalem. We wanted to use a platform of craft and the same central material – wood – in order to focus on empathy, tolerance, and acceptance of the Other. Additionally, a dialogue was triggered as to what is local design and how can we define cultural objects. We chose three distinct cultures of wood – South and West Africa, traditional Japanese philosophies and religions, and the Shakers – to trigger the students' own reflections towards empathy and tolerance while reflecting on the exterior and inherently different cultures. In the following pages, we will present three projects chosen out of over 450 which were accumulated over a period of 12 years we have been teaching in this studio. These will showcase our pedagogical approach towards integrating empathy into a unique studio dealing with craft, contemporary design, and the cultural object.

From a pedagogic perspective, during the last 13 years and after over 450 projects presented during those years, we've been teaching this course various socio-political and cultural, as well as inter-disciplinary, changes that affected and reshaped its various outlines. First, we can identify a clear transition from industrial design to product design. While it surpasses the scope of this chapter to delve into the definitions of craft or new craft, we see a clear shift from a traditional industrial design approach to a more flexible product-oriented practice. Thus, while in the early years, function was a key feature, it took a lesser prominent role in favour of reflection and empathy. While the first stage of our developed design process has been and still is cultural (social, philosophical, or religious) attributes, rituals, and belief systems, the lesser rows of the hierarchical ladder switched between aesthetics, interpretation, and classic designerly ways of knowing.[4] Second, as a department, the focus on inclusive design and empathetic design has seeped into this course as well. Therefore, understanding the Other led students to reflect upon their own realities. Lastly, from a pedagogical perspective, we can identify an ever-growing interest in the students' works to question their own beliefs and understandings of the world and go deeper than the mere fascination with Japanese culture, for example. This is understandable from a socio-political point of view, as local culture is going through a turbulent decade, vying to exterminate liberal thought and the acceptance of difference and pluralism. Some of the topics that resurface throughout these years and projects are contemporary Judaism, the role of women in society, religious re-interpretations, the individual versus social institutions, speculative design, belief systems, and one's influence on our daily lives. Out of all the works presented over the years, we chose just a handful to illustrate these complex dialogues.

Palestinian Femininity

Hadassah Academic College is situated in Jerusalem and as such offers many possibilities to examine the intricacies of Israeli social groups and cultures. Ultra-Orthodox, Settlers, Reformed Jews, Ethiopian Immigrants, Muslims, Christians, and more are all situated around the college and throughout the various neighbourhoods of Jerusalem. These intricate identities create an interesting and unique tapestry of material and visual culture. One such example was designed by Bassom Sakallah, who created a series of Palestinian jewellery based on her grandmother's heirloom, mixed with African techniques. Naturally, the material objects of every culture mirror its norms, traditions, and history. In addition to being a material manifestation of local and national identity, Palestinian jewellery, especially those made of silver and gold, has turned women into economic agents. For example, Nablus and Ramallah have long histories of manufacturing gold and silver jewellery for local communities, as well as for neighboring countries.[5] Furthermore, in the 20th century, gold jewellery has been used among Palestinian communities as a dowry signifying a family's wealth, while also serving as a form of moveable inheritance for the women of the family.[6]

One local Palestinian form of jewellery is a set of bracelets and a headband adorned with silver coins, on which local and religious sayings or verses are inscribed. The typical Palestinian festive outfit includes several items, such as *alssaffa* (a headband decorated with 80 silver or gold coins, common in Ramallah), *altaftaf* (a necklace comprising silver or gold coins, common in and around Jerusalem), or *alssamada* (a facial ornament, fastened beneath the woman's chin, typically worn by married women and marked by an abundance of gold coins), besides many other forms of jewellery.[7] Naturally, the fabrics, designs, and materials change according to region, national identity, and social belonging (northern or central Palestinians, Bedouins, etc.), as well as according to the woman's marital status.

In order to redesign this Palestinian jewellery set, imbuing it with one of the course's three main cultures of wood, designer Bassom Sakallah turned to the Ethiopian Hamar tribe, whose women wear a leather necklace around their necks. While most married women wear a simple one, called *esente*, the first wife in every household wears a more ornate one, with a protruding piece reminiscent of the male member, called *bignere*.[8] This necklace, along with their famous ochre body paint, distinguishes Hamar women from the women of neighbouring tribes.[9]

To create a woman's marital-status jewellery set, combining Hamar and Palestinian cultures, Sakallah combined olive and mahogany timbers, symbolizing each culture, using a stack-lamination technique. The first object is the Hassnah headband, adorned with a wooden version of the classic Palestinian silver coins, attesting to the family's wealth. The name of the object ('pretty girl' in Arabic) relates to its use by young single women, hence the lack of gold or ornamentation. The leather and the geometric patterning of the coins (beads in the original Hamar version) hint at the African design influence (Figure 3.1).

The second object, the Haram necklace, is based on the same techniques as the headband; yet, its aesthetics hints at an even-deeper connection with the Ethiopian Hamar tribe. Following Hamar custom, this necklace is meant

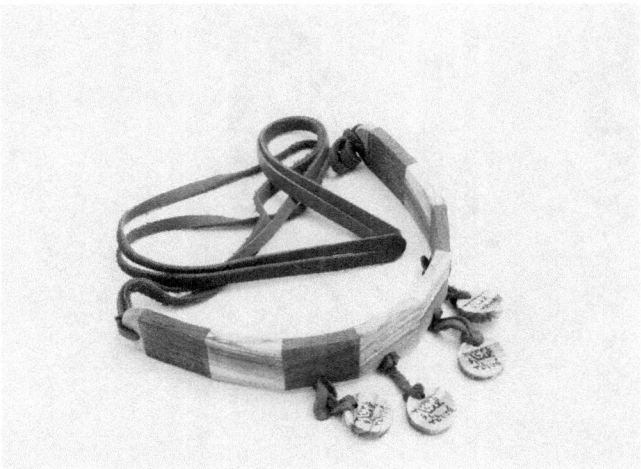

Figure 3.1 The Hassnah headband.

for soon-to-be-married women. In addition to its functional and ergonomic considerations, the geometric facets of the necklace reflect the design of the square beads of the Hamar, while also symbolizing the end of childhood and the awakening of femininity. The name of the necklace, 'the wife of' in Arabic, attests to its use for signifying a married woman, hence its abundance of coins. Again, the combination of olive and mahogany timbers highlights the mixture of the two different cultures' views on marriage and femininity (Figures 3.2 and 3.3).

Improvisation and Mastery

There are not many intriguing and complex cultures equal to Japan. Flexible in its fluid religious attitude, poetic yet full of historical cruelty, and gentle yet abrupt, its uniqueness offers a rare opportunity to mirror and highlight one's own faults and perplexities. Indeed, at first glance, there could not be two cultures more different than the Israeli and the Japanese, both in general and particularly regarding design. While the latter holds patience, reflection, years-old tradition, and attention to a product in its minuscule details, the former is highly erratic, arrogant, aggressive, and short-sighted. These cultural differences are clearly reflected when dealing with the culture of wood, a material that demands respect, patience, and meticulous planning. While an Israeli craftsperson would make do with what lies around their studio, their Japanese counterpart would take care to follow the ways of the trade, its traditions, and the teachings of former masters and honoured thinkers. Taking these differences in stride, designer

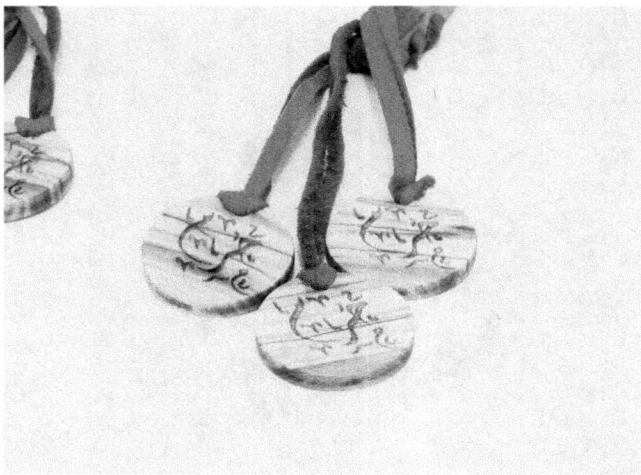

Figure 3.2 Wooden decorative coins.

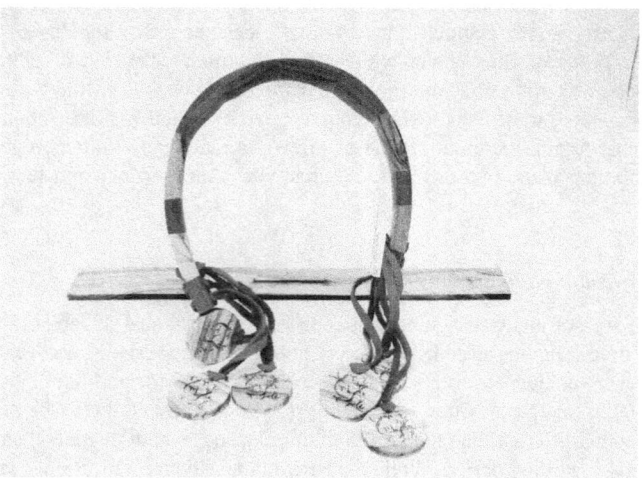

Figure 3.3 The Haram necklace.

Kfir Zada-Cohen designed two sets of tools for the master of wood, one mirroring Israeli craft ideologies and the other, their Japanese equivalents.

Carpenters hold a unique liminal position in Japanese culture, standing on the threshold between modern technology (*gijutsu*), mass production, architecture and design, and traditional Japanese ethics and philosophy of craft. At the pinnacle of this traditional craft stands the *daiku*, or master carpenter. Among other things, their craft and traditional knowledge saved these *daiku* from extinction during the Meiji reforms of the 1870s. The term *daiku* ('great artisan') meant a master artisan in general; yet during the Edo period (1600–1868), it came to refer to professionals who constructed architecture from wood. Indeed, the *daiku* were far from a small elite, for, during this period, a third of all Edo artisans were considered *daiku*. Therefore, prefixes were added to designate and differentiate between areas of expertise: *miya-daiku* built temples, *sukiya-daiku* built teahouses and residential housing for samurai and *ie-daiku* built regular urban houses, while un-prefixed *daiku* built rural ones. Later on, however, during the last years of the shogunate, the term *daiku* came to designate a master carpenter, while, following the Meiji reforms, the term architect naturally took over as a designation for professionals building houses and other structures. Since most Japanese structures were made of wood, a master carpenter enjoyed great respect and prestige.[10]

Following this unique perception of the *daiku*, Zada-Cohen juxtaposed two design ideologies. On the one hand, the traditional Japanese artisan imbues his actions with a premeditated philosophy, paying attention to every detail, paying tribute to his tools of the trade and every material used, and bringing to fruition hundreds of years of professionalism and tradition. On the other hand, the Israeli image of the master carpenter depicts a somewhat contradictory image of a repairperson, excelling in 'handling' problems on the fly through improvisation tactics, which might lead to unexpected innovation. The result is two sets of tools, one for the Japanese craftsperson and the other, for their Israeli counterpart. Each series includes three typical and traditional carpentry tools: a mallet (usually used with a set of chisels, when working on joinery parts), a hand plane, and a marking gauge:

- *The mallet*: The Japanese mallet is made of three types of timber (the handle is made of oak, and the head, of a combination of maple and cherry) to increase accuracy, precision, and strength. The mallet's head is joined by a special joinery technique called scarf joint. The Israeli mallet is made of recycled beech joined by a simple t-shaped metal tube, found in every repairperson's garage. The head of the mallet is filled with washer bolts to enhance its weight, a cheap and easy solution.
- *The hand plane*: The Japanese version is an example of the precision and mastery of its carpentry tradition. Its lower half is made of maple, symbolizing harmony, while the upper half is made of cherry, symbolizing innovation and growth. The wedge is made of oak, a symbol of strength and stability. The two parts are joined using a special type of swallowtail joinery. The Israeli version is an emblem of improvisation and the use of found materials and objects. While the base of the hand plane

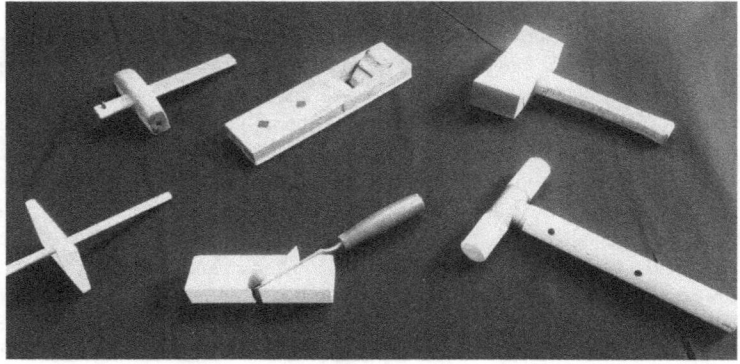

Figure 3.4 Israeli improvisation (lower row) and Japanese mastery (upper row).

is made of a leftover piece of maple timber, the mouth of the plane is made of a ready-made chisel. The result is a highly functional, cheap, and easy-to-make object.

• *The marking gauge*: A marking gauge is an object used to measure three-dimensional cuts precisely, usually utilized in joinery and cabinet-making. The Japanese marking gauge follows the exact traditional proportions of the object, using a combination of maple, cherry, and oak. The Israeli equivalent is a highly reductionist version of its Japanese counterpart and is made of three parts: a maple plane with an inserted beech screw anchor, completed with a simple nail, used to scratch the wood to mark the precise cutting line.

While perhaps less sophisticated in its use of materials and techniques, the Israeli series is highly innovative in finding cheaper and quicker solutions. Embodying the Israeli attitude of 'getting the job done', this series is no less interesting or functional than its Japanese counterpart. This project mirrors the complexity of Israeli professional existence. While we crave for an honourable and culturally rooted tradition, we confess in our relatively young material origins and almost revel in our ability to prosper under duress with a short supply of options and materials. While potentially leading to jaw-dropping innovation, it might end in disaster (Figures 3.4–3.7).

African-Japanese De Stijl

Without delving too deep into the intricate subject of post-Colonialism, comparing various countries governed by the British Government, we wish to highlight a unique project raising the question of appropriation and design canon (Figure 3.8). While asking the students if anyone can name

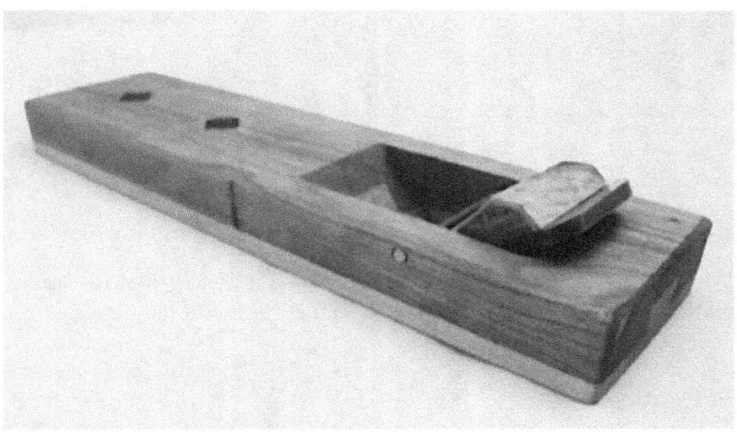

Figure 3.5 The Japanese hand plane, notice the elegant and culturally accurate joinery techniques on the upper left part and the right part of this piece.

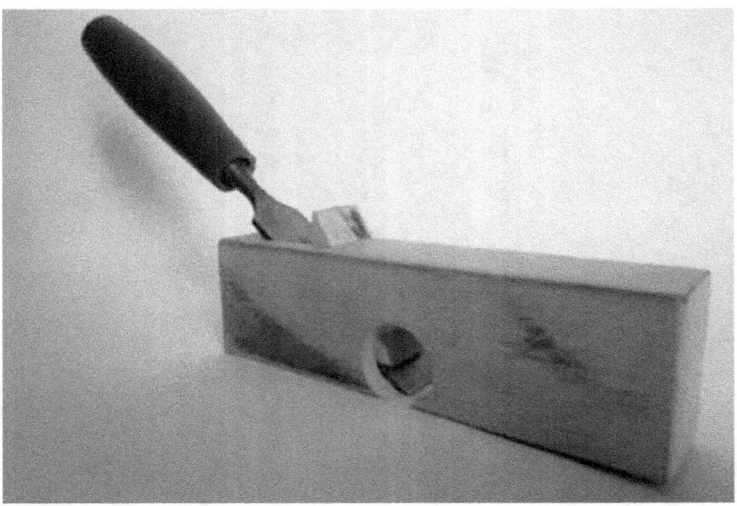

Figure 3.6 The Israeli hand plane.

an African-native designer or architect (receiving an echoing silence), they all know the Bauhaus and its historical counterparts in detail. Naturally, as parts of Tel Aviv were built in the style of the Bauhaus, other Western design traditions are prominent in the design curriculum around the world. Gerrit

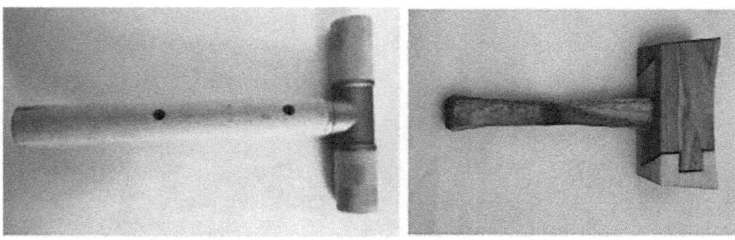

Figure 3.7 The Israeli mallet, depicting a classic T-shaped tubing (left) and the Japanese mallet, showcasing a beautiful joinery technique (right).

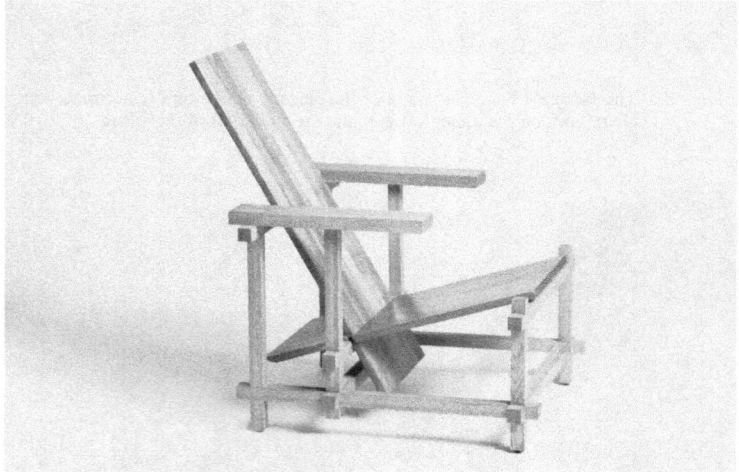

Figure 3.8 Afro-Japanese Rietveld.

Rietveld's *Red and Blue Chair* is one of the most famous design pieces and a herald of De Stijl in particular and modern design in general. While De Stijl's universality promoted basic colours and geometric forms, as a countermeasure to the national differentiation that led to the horrific human loss during the First World War, it also left room for individuality.[11] Rietveld's declared intention was to design an affordable chair, made of machine-cut plywood and put together by dowels and glue, demanding no element of craftsmanship. While the chair is almost a sculptural or architectural exercise, its function seems almost offhanded, and even Rietveld himself complained of bruising his ankles while using it.[12] The chair is made of two systems: painted planes that support the body and black panels that support them.[13] This universal,

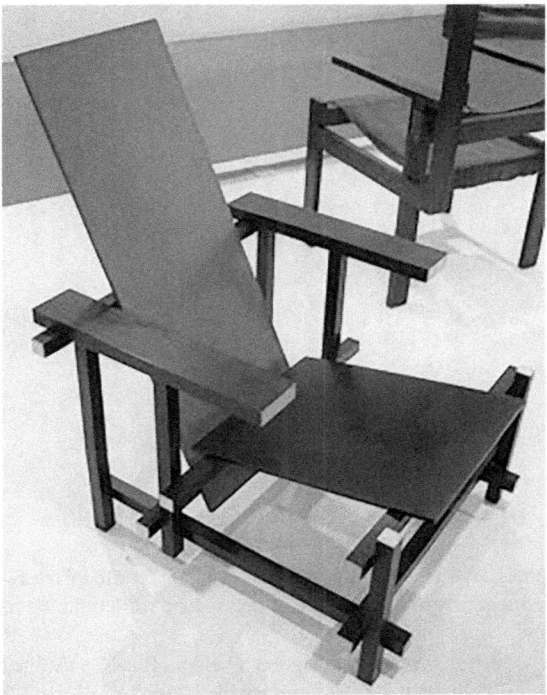

Figure 3.9 Red and Blue Chair, Gerrit Riefveld, 1917.

yet individualistic approach paved the way for the design of our next object, integrating De Stijl, African furniture, and Japanese joinery.

Japanese joinery workers take a somewhat similar architectural approach in creating a lean, structural, almost-engineered frame, which is not only functional but also beautiful in its intricacy. So important was this unique knowledge of assembling buildings and furniture without nails or screws, that these craftsmen were called *sashimono* ('fitted things').[14] One of the influences of Zen on cabinetmaking is the essence of unseen beauty, characterized by the intelligent use of joinery (Figure 3.9).

In contradistinction, furniture making in the classic African tradition calls for the use of derogation, much like the imagination of a sculptor bringing to life a marble figure through the exclusion of all the extra material. In many African tribes, social hierarchy is materialized through the design of each individual's chair. While each chair would usually be built to support its user's body in a low, reclining, close-to-the-ground posture, the chief's chair would be designed in such a manner as to stand out as the highest in the room. One of

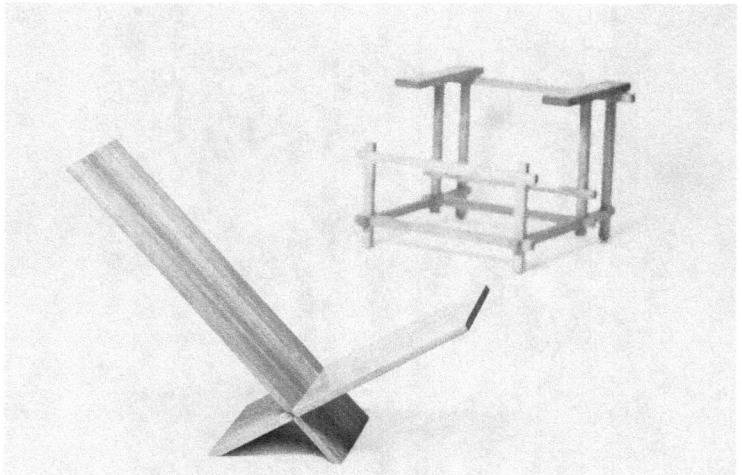

Figure 3.10 The African (front) and De-Stijl (back) parts of the chair.

the most famous African chairs is the Malawi chair, crafted from two pieces of wood joined together to create a reclining posture while maintaining strength and stability.

As can be seen in this chair, designed by Noam Bar-Shalev, the redesign of the classic Rietveld chair brings together the handicraft of the African chair, coupled with Japanese joinery and De Stijl simplicity and austere aesthetics. Contrary to the original Rietveld design, in this chair, the various parts are constructed without any screws or glue, as is customary in the Japanese way of *sashimono*. Similarly, the two parts are originally joined together in the classic African manner. By elegantly joining these three design cultures, the essence of De Stijl becomes even clearer, since the simplicity of construction is evident; yet, an elusive sense of individuality remains hidden, only to be revealed to an expert eye. This is a unique example of a post-colonial approach highlighting a combination of several cultures, while intentionally erasing the historical hierarchies between the three. As a result, this project asks other pertinent questions – what is design canon? Can or should we question it? What is vernacular design in a globally similar visual-material reality? (Figure 3.10).

African Tefillin

Designing a dialogue between cultures brings forth a unique type of interpretation, one that also questions each culture's perceptions and conventions. Judaism, as a very rigid religious system, offers another layer of interpretation when mixed with other cultural frameworks. Indeed, the *Tefillin* is a famous example. On every morning (except Saturdays), one sees temporary marks on the left arm of every orthodox Jewish male over the age of 13. These are made by the leather strips of the *tefillin*, comprising a pair of small boxes, one of which is placed on the upper left arm (facing the heart), while the other is placed on the head. The act of wearing the *tefillin* professes the wearer's belief in the Torah, God, and the exodus out of Egypt. By placing one of the *tefillin* above the brain and the other facing the heart, observing Jews declare that both heart and mind are subject to God; therefore, the *tefillin* are also called *ot*, meaning 'sign' in Hebrew. In the first project, we will present a *tefillin*-related project, which is a redesign of the *tefillin* influenced by African rites of passage. This is an interesting approach towards religious tolerance and empathy, as this shift from Judaism to pagan local African religion strictly prohibited to observing Jews.

Each *tefillin* outer case is a box made of leather, 2–4 centimetres in size, covering another, smaller box called the *titora*. While the arm *tefillin* is smooth, the head *tefillin* has the letter שׁ (*shin*, the first letter of God's name in Hebrew) marked on two of its sides, one with three branches and the other with four. The boxes are hollow and contain four verses (*parshiyot*) from the Torah inscribed on parchments. While in the arm *tefillin*, all four verses are inscribed on a single parchment, in the head *tefillin*, each is inscribed on a separate one. While the arm *tefillin* contains a single hollow opening, the head *tefillin* contains four small compartments, into which each of the parchments is inserted. The four verses are 'Sanctify to me…' (Exod. 13:1–10 KJV); 'When God brings you…' (13:11–16); 'Hear, O Israel…' (Deut. 6:4–9 KJV); and 'If you observe My Commandments…' (11:13–21). A designated scribe

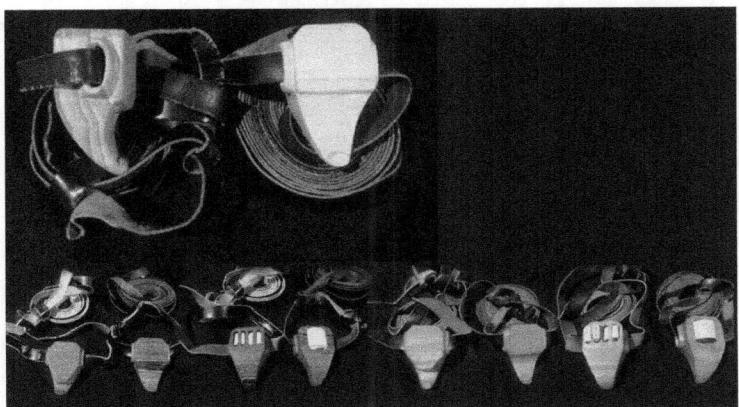

Figure 3.11 Miki Untberg's African tefillin.

(*sofer stam*) writes the verses with special ink, following the same purity rules as when writing the Torah or a *mezuzah* (Figure 3.11).[15]

The design of the African *tefillin* combines the traditional wooden masks of the Lwalwa tribe from the eastern part of the Democratic Republic of the Congo and the three main rites of passage conducted by orthodox male Jews: circumcision (*brit milah*, conducted eight days after birth); bar mitzvah (conducted at the age of 13 to symbolize a boy's transition into manhood); and, finally, marriage (the gateway to raising a new family). Each set of *tefillin* is symbolizes one of these consecutive rites of passage, mirrored by the increasingly darker timber used for it. Conversely, in Africa masks symbolize a range of different meanings and have many functions. In the Lwalwa tribe, a central use of local masks is the guidance of teens during their coming-of-age ceremony. The mask carvers in this tribe – in many cases, the local village chief – enjoy great prestige and oversee ritualistic dances. These dances are associated with the Ngongo, a group responsible for the initiation and circumcision rituals of young boys, meant to appease the spirits. There are four known types of masks, and each person commissions their favourite from the local carver. The tribe's masks are minimalistic and geometric in their design, portraying the bare features of male or female facial attributes, such as eye slits and a long, distinctive nose. These are usually made of local mulela timber.[16]

The Lwalwa *tefillin*, designed by Miki Onterberg, were aesthetically based on these traditional masks, using the same carving techniques. Three types of timber were used to create a graduation of increasingly darker wood: African walnut, mahogany, and wenge. In an innovative fashion, the two cultures' rites of passage accumulate in this set of *tefillin*. As the boy grows, his *tefillin*'s craft echoes his new social status and entry into the socio-cultural group. The cultural significance of this project surpasses its aesthetics. First, the very comparison between Judaism and Local Lwalwa paganism creates a cultural thread, asking for similarities. Second, the notion that rites of passage, as an anthropologic common denominator to all human societies, are quickly becoming innovative, especially so in a segregated cultural system, such as Judaism.

The Ethos of Beauty

Throughout the years, two interconnected issues kept resurfacing, challenging contemporary norms and conventions of both Israeli and Jewish traditions – the role of women in Israeli religious and secular societies, and culturally determined body classifications vis-à-vis the very definition of beauty and physical aesthetics. In her classic book *The Beauty Myth* (2002), Naomi Wolf highlights the culturally oriented definition of feminine beauty in Western society. The culturally embedded norm of feminine beauty, accordingly, is a result of patriarchal conventions embedded in Western society, culminating in contemporary consumer culture and popular media. Famously, Wolf stresses that beauty is viewed as an objective goal women must embody, while men have to possess these model women. Griselda Pollock[17] demonstrated the depiction of femininity and the role of objectifying women for the enjoyment of spectators (men, of course) in art history.[18] Obviously, delving into the various aspects of embodiment and the theoretical aspects of power and the body is beyond our capacities in this volume,[19] nonetheless, we will shed light on several issues regarding the body and femininity. Consumer culture turned the feminine body into an unnatural and technologically moulded type unreachable and separated from the 'normal' body. The image of the young, slim, muscular body consisting of 0% fat became the global norm, evoking large breasts, a slim waistline, and a flat stomach.[20] Indeed, a key understanding throughout this course was the link between Botox injections or cosmetic surgeries and the traditional blackened teeth of women in Japan, or the scarification rituals of various tribes in South and West Africa.

A central materialization of such feminine bodily perceptions can be seen in dolls, especially in the case of Barbie. Following various researchers, we can clearly see that Barbie's body is unrealistic, unnatural, and unattainable; yet, it remains the best-selling doll (albeit haphazard superficial attempts by Mattel to change this perception), influencing the body images of men, women, and children alike. As is the case with many other toys and especially with dolls, children report dissatisfaction with their body image after playing with these.[21] Mattel, which builds and manufactures Barbie, has sent several child models across the US appealing to 'get in shape' as Barbie. Furthermore, some of the most important features of Barbie are her accessories, ranging from makeup and hairdos to bags and clothes, broadcasting a distinct and exact mode of femininity and sexuality.[22] The result is a Western depiction of feminine beauty, specifically distributed in various media; Barbie is all-influencing in her plasticity and global appeal,[23] in her manifestation as an almost posthuman technological entity (Figure 3.12).[24]

In this project, designed by Hila Raam, we can see an abstract materialization of three models of femininity, based on a more flexible definition of the term. The famous Western depiction of feminine beauty is the classic 60–90–60 figure, depicted, among other things, in the Barbie doll and countless ads and commercials. Conversely, the ideal feminine beauty in Japan calls for long, shiny black hair, white skin, and a slender physique.[25],[26] Alternately, the classic African feminine model, as seen in various art pieces and archaeological figurines, boasts large breasts and bottom, echoing fertility and health.[27] In this project, the platform of *kokeshi* dolls is used to illustrate and question such inherent cultural depictions of feminine beauty. One such question revolves around 'is there indeed a feminine ethos of beauty and who decides', as another centred on 'is our own culture better or more coherent than others'.

Following the classic craft of the *kokeshi*, each doll is made of four parts (head, torso, waist, and legs), along with the traditional size of the *kokeshi*.

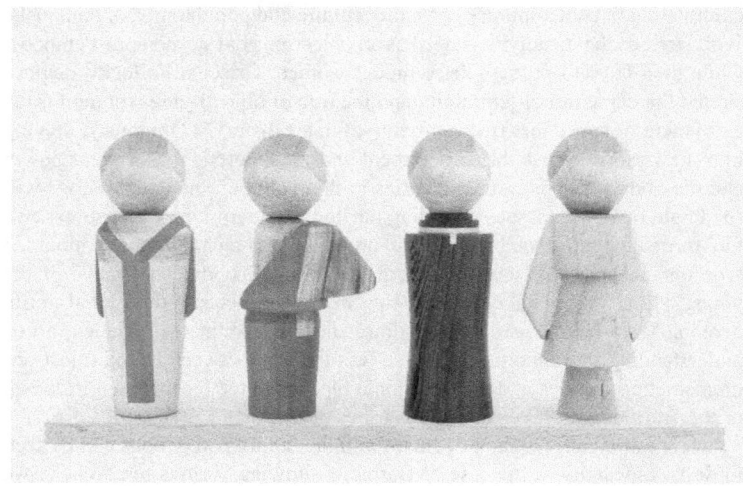

Figure 3.12 Three models of beauty: Japanese (left), African (centre), and Western (right).

The Japanese doll, made of maple, depicts classic Japanese beauty: long and slender features, a flat chest, and pale skin. The maple adds not only paleness but also the general flawlessness of its grain, further accentuating the pursuit of flawless skin in Japanese tradition. The African doll exhibits generous breasts, bottom, and waist. This *kokeshi* is made of walnut, a darker tree rich with grain features and natural ornamentation, alluding to African tribal painting and scarification. The American (Western) doll depicts a muscular, statuesque, and somewhat unnatural physique. The slender waist, large breasts, smaller head, and muscular legs are further accentuated by the unnatural tan of the reddish eucalyptus. The playful element of mixing the three dolls alludes to the arbitrariness of beauty judgements and our own definition of beauty vis-à-vis other cultures (Figure 3.13).

Learning Tolerance through the Fluidity of Japanese Religious Attitude

As the years went by and the course evolved, we found new ways to highlight and embed inclusive design through cultural artefacts. A crucial strategy, as we have seen, was the starting point of estranging the students' own culture, while developing a sense of empathy and tolerance towards other cultures. Naturally, critical thinking and political design helped in taking this modus operandi even further. Indeed, a topic that resurfaced many times was

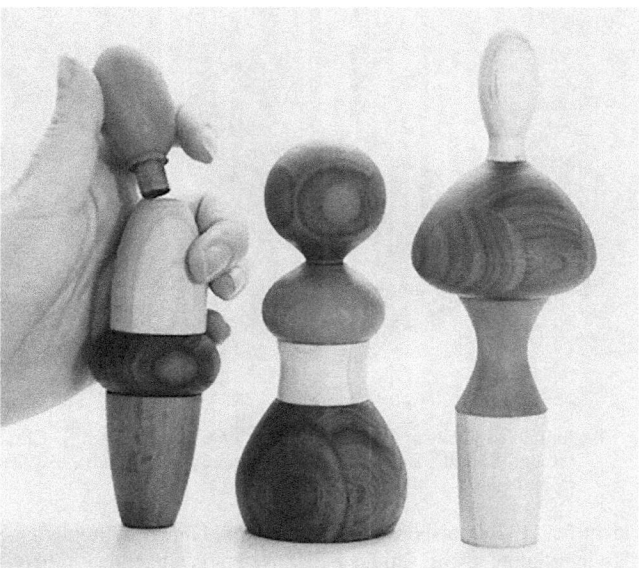

Figure 3.13 The three feminine figures through a mix-and-max scenario.

Judaism's classic understanding as a very rigid religion and its problematic view of the Other. In stark contrast, one of Japan's most unique attributes is its tolerance towards non-vernacular religions. Conversely, three of the central religions in Japan are not indigenous. According to the US Department of State, 51% of Japanese identify with Shinto belief, 34% are Buddhists, and a meagre 2% are Christians.[28] However, a person in Japan can believe in two sets of faiths, unlike Judaism, for instance, in which the faithful have to be exclusively Jewish. Religious tolerance and freedom of belief are rooted in the essence of the state, taking precedence over all else.[29] In this sense, it is understandable that Christianity did not take root in Japan due to its exclusivist ethos. Indeed, during the 17th century, Christianity was banned in Japan, after enjoying a new-found tolerance prior to the Meiji reforms (Figure 3.14).[30]

The history of these four religions and their impact on Japan reflects Japanese origins and culture. Indigenous in nature, Shinto ('way of the gods') is one of the two central religions in Japan, boasting around 100,000 shrines and 20,000 priests, who are recognized for their unique attire. The earliest records of Shinto date back to the 6th century, and it survives as a socio-cultural complex and a practised religion today. The above-mentioned religious flexibility can be seen in the fact that, while Shinto is the largest religion in Japan, supported by around 100 million citizens, only a small percentage of

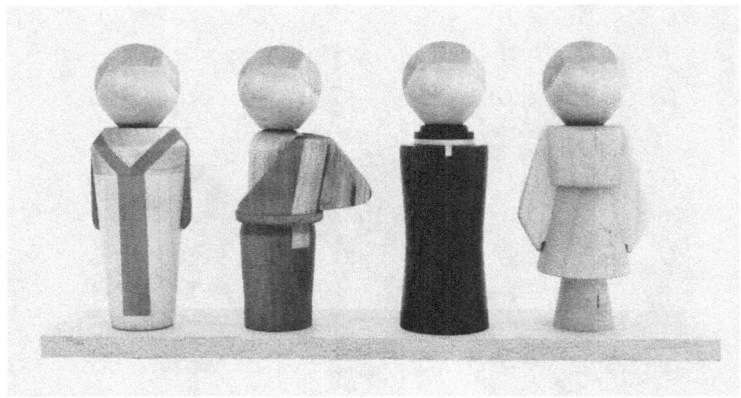

Figure 3.14 Religious-pluralism kokeshi: Shinto (first from the right), Christianity
(second from the right), Buddhism (second from the left), and Dao (first
from the left).

them identifies as Shintoists. Conversely, it would be wrong to define Shinto
as a classic religion, as this unique belief system is embedded in history and
practice alike, including shrine rituals (since *kami* reside in shrines), as well
as holidays and festivals.[31]

Unlike Shinto, Daoism (or Taoism) and Buddhism are not indigenous to
Japan. Dao was brought to Japan from China as a philosophical and religious
method for reaching the Way. The roots of Daoism go back as far as the 4th–2nd
centuries BCE.[32] This Chinese belief system was developed between the
2nd and 6th centuries CE revolving around the writings of Lao Tzu (especially his famous *Tao Te Ching*). While contemporary Daoism consists of
an almost-endless variation of approaches, its central ethos revolves around
reaching insight through one's self.[33] Daoism is hard to define because it has
never been united under one rule. In addition, Chinese religion is a mixture
of three teachings (Buddhism, Confucianism, and Daoism). While in China
Taoism and Confucianism are related, in contemporary Japan, this is not the
case, and indeed few would identify themselves as Daoist. Buddhism was
introduced to Japan much later. The first official record, the Korean king Song
Myong sending an image of the Buddha along with several sutras, dates to
538; yet, researchers claim that Buddhism reached Japan much earlier through
unofficial channels. Prince Shotoku (574–622) studied Buddhism, erected
shrines, and is considered the father of Japanese Buddhism.[34]

The basic configuration of the figurines designed by Harel Oberman follows the dimensions and proportions of the classic *kokeshi* doll. Their head
is similar and made of cherry, while the bodies vary according to each of the
principal Japanese religions. The Shinto *kokeshi* is made of maple and follows
the abstract shape of Shinto-priest robes; the maple echoing the white fabric.

The Catholic *kokeshi* is identified by the distinguished white collar and black clothes, made of wenge timber. The Buddhist *kokeshi* depicts the characteristic asymmetric orange robes, leaving the right shoulder bare. The doll is made of a combination of maple and red eucalyptus. Finally, the Dao *kokeshi* echoes the ornate and flowing robes of Daoist monks and is made of eucalyptus and cherry. An added layer of tolerance is understood by the lack of hierarchy when viewing the kokeshi side-by-side.

Ultra-Orthodox Netsuke

As we have a seen, a culturally rooted object can serve as a platform to broadcast a new interpretation on one's own society. Like the *kokeshi*, *netsuke* – an ornate figurine meant to hold the Japanese equivalent of a purse (*inro*) attached to the person's belt – can serve as a platform for re-interpreting broad cultural norms and values. As the history and socio-cultural aspects of the Japanese *netsuke* surpass the scope of this article, suffice to say, these minute objects served functional (securing a person's *oni* or purse on their belt) and social (status, identity, etc.) purposes. Furthermore, *netsuke* hold various symbolic meanings, relating to Buddhist or Shinto beliefs, social norms, folklore maxims, and more. In other words, *netsuke* are a material mirror of Japanese daily life. The symbolic value of *netsuke*, therefore, is almost limitless, ranging from Zen monks to pseudo-pornographic imagery and blurring the boundaries between reality and fantasy. However, the most popular themes are based on legends, religion and mythology, with the later addition of daily scenes and literary inspirations during the 19th century.[35]

As our interpretations of *netsuke* do not stem from any functional need, their design can be related to vernacular symbolism, if the overall material rules (regarding height, material, etc.) are kept. From this perspective, the relationship between Japanese and Hasidic symbolism might seem natural, and some researchers identify various links between Shinto and Judaism (see, for example, Shillony[36]). Besides a common history of exclusion, racism, and a complex interaction with Christianity, both Jews and Japanese share various theological and philosophical traits. Although Shinto is much more accommodating towards other religions than Judaism, we find common tenets regarding purity, the family and the strength of one's community as a cohesive social-cultural unit (Figure 3.15).

Another common trait relevant to both traditions is the inner social segregation apparent in the material and visual code of clothing and accessories. These considerations, among others, led to the redesign of the *netsuke,* fusing its traditional Japanese design with Hasidic culture. Representing modesty, frugality and asceticism, daily ultra-orthodox Jewish menswear includes a black suit, a hat and a white buttoned shirt. On Saturdays (Shabbat), the suit is replaced by a silk or satin caftan, along with a luxurious fur hat. The black colour signifies piety and unanimous collectivism and serves as a reminder

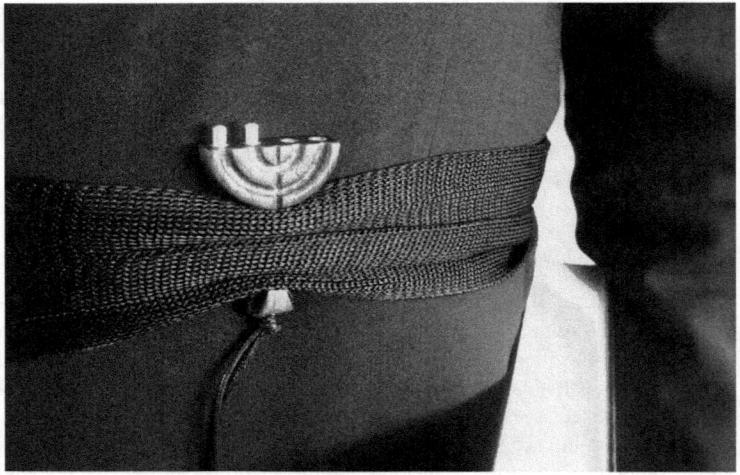

Figure 3.15 Ziv Shriki's ultra-orthodox netsuke.

of the destruction of the second Temple, as well as acting as a functional 'boundary marker' to establish a clear and univocal binary opposition of 'us' and 'them'.

As in other cultures, Haredi (ultra-orthodox) clothing is a manifestation of political and religious affiliations, as well as a mirror of one's wealth, position, and marital status. The Hasidic *gartel* (belt) is usually woven from black silk thread, ending with loose strings, but albeit its specific cultural significance, it resembles the Japanese *obi*, on which the *Inrō* and *netsuke* were hung. Therefore, in this project, designed by Ziv Shriki, the material distinction between the various Haredi factions is accurately defined, pinpointing specific sub-groups in Jerusalem. As we saw earlier, since *netsuke* symbolism is open to interpretation, its use as a material platform imbued with Haredi symbolism was a good starting point for this project. The result is a series of Haredi *netsuke*, each embedded in and symbolizing one Hasidic court, differentiated by its colours, symbols, and imagery. Again, in this example, while contrasting two seemingly different groups in a single designed artefact, the student (an ultra-orthodox herself) opened to the significant cultural similarities and reflected upon the contributions each culture and religion could offer.

Political Satire – Afro-Israeli Political Masks

As in other young countries rife with conflict and political turmoil, political debates may offer another venue for learning empathy and acceptance. Add to this mixture two more explosive socio-political elements – an immigrant culture and one that was ruled by foreign empires throughout history – and individuals' complex and sceptical relation to their political leaders becomes a bit understandable. As we all know, facial features have various manifestations in art and other cultural-material and visual representations. In modern Western Europe, leaders' facial features served as a pincushion for political satire and caricature, offering a visual, mass-produced means of letting off citizens' political steam. In contrast to Western European caricaturists' depictions of their leaders, in Africa in general, and specifically among the Dogon, ritualistic wooden masks capture and enhance the leader's energy, strength, and authoritarian power. Laughter at other people's expense has always been a part of the human experience. However, when put to paper, visual representations of people (and later – of political figures) using caricature and satire became a hallmark of the modern era. When coined in Italy in 1590, the word caricature referred to a type of exaggerated portrait. In the 1590s, the brothers Agostino and Annibale Carracci started creating pen drawings of distorted human heads. While their original drawings did not survive, it is clear from their descriptions that humoristic features were key. Naturally, not until the technological and professional innovations of the Renaissance did caricature artists learn how to enhance this new style. In fact, Italian sculptor Bernini was known for amusing his friends with caricature drawings.[37]

Among art historians and theoreticians, it was the renowned Ernst Gombrich[38] who turned the academic spotlight onto caricature:

> It is a startling fact that portrait caricature was not known to the world before the end of the sixteenth century. What seems too simple and even primitive to us, the conscious distortion of the features of a person with the aim of ridicule, was not even attempted in classical antiquity nor in the Middle Ages or the Renaissance. Artists of these former periods were very well acquainted with comic art in general… The reason why the methods evolved by the first caricaturists of the seventeenth century did not lose their vigour but lived on in modern caricature lies in the fact that they set in motion certain psychic mechanisms which, since those days, have always formed the essence of the caricature's effect.

At the heart of this project, by designer Elad Herman, stands the question, 'how would caricatures of famous Israeli leaders look if they were Dogon masks?' (Figure 3.16). As in other projects presented in this chapter, the method of estrangement allows the students to 'use' other cultures to evaluate and criticize their own culture from a distanced position. Following the traditional Dogon mask design suggested a specific configuration, whose basic attributes are geometric lines and abstract facial features. Israeli politics is characterized by constant change and fluidity. Last year's leaders often run again after changing the name of their party or representing an altogether different one, as power and influence take precedence over loyalty and values.

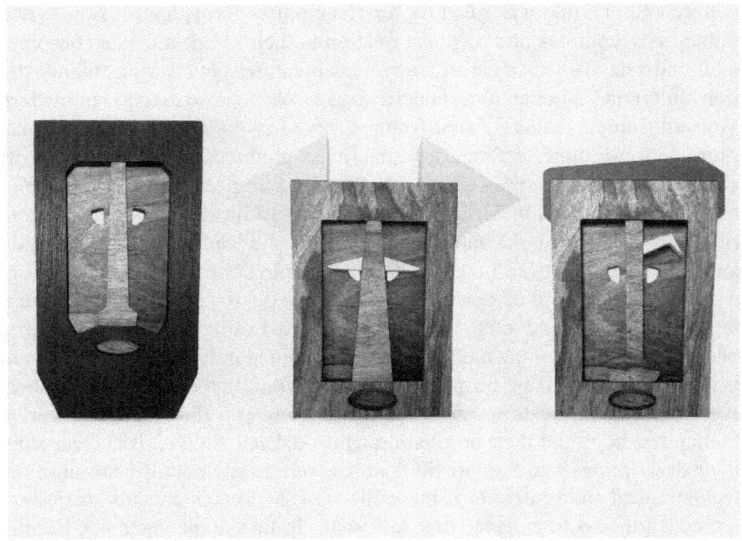

Figure 3.16 Elad Herman's caricaturist masks – Theodor Herzl (L), David Ben Gurion (C), and Binyamin Netanyahu (R).

This led to the design of interchangeable masks, enabling a 'mix-and-match' usage. The Dogon, currently situated in northern Mali, relocated from the banks of the Niger to the adjacent hilly areas to escape slave traders from Ghana. While their tribal religion and rituals are rife with mystery and were initially not fully understood by Westerners, French anthropologist Marcel Griaule (1898–1956) shed some light on several vastly interesting aspects. Among these rituals is the mysterious ceremony called *sigi*. During it, which takes place once every 60 years, the Great Mask (the mother of masks) is carved anew. The Great Mask, depicting a flat snake and eyes extends approximately 9 meters into the air and is kept in a secret cave known only to a few. The mask represents the first death and the ensuing life force (*nyama*) in the world. Interestingly, while the Dogon did not possess a written language, they had an intricate and highly sophisticated system of symbols, whose philosophical layout, consisting of cosmology and metaphysics, was first identified by Griaule.[39] Notably, the Dogon religion has some similarities to Judaism, ancient Egyptian rites, and Buddhism. For example, the Dogon circumcise their young, wears skullcaps and prayer shawls, and observe a jubilee year.[40]

To design the Dogon-based caricature masks of Israeli political leaders, designer Elad Herman chose one specific type out of 78 possible configurations. It is an abstract rectangular mask featuring geometric lines and distinctive eye sockets. The frame of the mask is modular, allowing its basic configuration to be modified into three distinct portraits of prominent Israeli leaders – Theodor Herzl, David Ben-Gurion, and Benjamin Netanyahu. These were chosen due to their distinctive features and cultural importance. Herzl is identified by his thick black beard and old-fashioned hairstyle, Ben-Gurion, by his shock of grey hair, and Netanyahu by his thinning, purple-tinged hair. The dynamic configuration of the mask mirrors the temporary nature of Israeli politics, which often sees unexpected political changes during each govern-ment term. The masks were cut by CNC and built according to the rules of traditional Japanese joinery. The timber chosen for the project was maple, African walnut, wenge, and purpleheart. Indeed, while far from holy, these representations of political leaders hold a cultural mirror to our deepest hopes and fears. Returning to Rousseau's opening statement, we are always looking for a leader who can help to release us from our collective chains.

In the last decade design culture has been interpreted differently by vari-ous researchers and practitioners. We want to emphasize that empathetic design holds the same potential. While it is typically associated with inclusive design, or healthcare and medical design, we believe that linking it to vernacu-lar design and design culture holds even more potential for embedding values in students' projects as an inherent part of our pedagogic mission. As we have seen in these short examples, empathy is a crucial trait necessary to design students facing the intricate challenges to come. By opting to integrate empa-thy into less evident topics, such as carpentry or craft we raise an important flag. Designers should immerse themselves in current socio-cultural issues, raise critical thinking, and imbue in their students the ability to tackle wicked questions and offer necessary insight. In a way, while accomplishing this goal, as beautiful as they are, the final designed products may seem like just a good excuse to trigger a much-needed change.

Notes

1 Hassan Fathy, *Architecture for the Poor: An Experiment in Rural Egypt* (Chicago, IL: University of Chicago Press, 1973), 19.
2 Guy Julier, "From Visual Culture to Design Culture," *Design Issues* 22, no. 1 (2006): 65.
3 Ezio Manzini, "Design Culture and Dialogic Design," *Design Issues* 32, no. 1 (2016): 53.
4 Nigel Cross, *Designerly Ways of Knowing* (London: Springer, 2006).
5 Annelies Moors, "Wearing Gold," in *Border Fetishisms: Material Objects in Unsta-ble Spaces*, ed. Patricia Spyer (Abingdon: Routledge, 1998), 208.
6 Russell Rebecca Ross, *Gender and Jewelry: A Feminist Analysis* (Medford, MA: Tufts University, 2010).
7 https://bedouinsilver.com.
8 http://larskrutak.com/ethiopias-last-frontier-the-bloody-world-of-the-hamar-tribe.
9 Dima Nicholas, *Culture, Religion, and Geopolitics* (Xlibris Corporation, 2010); John, Markakis, *Ethiopia: The Last Two Frontiers*, Vol. 10 (Suffolk: Boydell & Brewer Ltd, 2011).

10 Azby Brown, *The Genius of Japanese Carpentry: Secrets of an Ancient Craft* (Rutland, VT: Tuttle, 2014); Gregory Clancey, "Modernity and Carpenters: Daiku Technique and Meiji Technocracy," in *Building a Modern Japan: Science, Technology and Medicine in the Meiji Era and Beyond*, ed. Morris Law (New York: Palgrave Macmillan, 2005), 183.

11 David Raizman, *History of Modern Design: Graphics and Products since the Industrial Revolution* (London: Laurence King, 2003).

12 Clement Meadmore, *The Modern Chair: Classic Designs by Thonet, Breuer, Le Corbusier, Eames and Others* (Mineola NY: Dover Publications, 2019).

13 Jim Postell, *Furniture Design* (London: John Wiley and Sons, 2012).

14 Kazuko Koizumi, *Traditional Japanese Furniture* (Tokyo: Kodansha international, 1986).

15 Shimon Eider, *Halachos of Tefillin* (Jerusalem: Feldheim, 1984); Moshe Neiman, *Tefillin: An Illustrated Guide to Their Makeup and Use* (Jerusalem: Feldheim, 1995).

16 Iris Hahner-Herzog, Maria Kecskesi and Lazlo Vajda, *African Masks: From the Barbier-Mueller Collection* (New York: Prestel, 2007), 121–5; Susan Vogel (Ed.), *For Spirits and Kings: African Art from the Paul and Ruth Tishman Collection* (New York: Metropolitan Museum of Art, 1981).

17 Griselda Pollock, *Vision and Difference: Femininity, Feminism and the Histories of Art* (Abingdon: Routledge, 1988).

18 Griselda Pollock, *Differencing the Canon: Feminism and the Writing of Art's Histories* (Abingdon: Routledge, 2013).

19 One good starting point, among many, would be the volume *Embodied Practices* (1997), ed. Kathy Davis.

20 Sarah Grogan, *Body Image: Understanding Body Dissatisfaction in Men, Women and Children*, 4th edition (Abingdon: Routledge, 2021).

21 Helga Ditmar, *Consumer Culture, Identity and Well-Being: The Search for the "Good Life" and the "Body Perfect"* (Hove and New York: Psychology Press).

22 Ingebord Majer O'Sickey, "Barbie Magazine and the Aesthetic Commodification of Girls' Bodies," in *On Fashion*, ed. Shari Benstock and Suzanne Ferriss (New Brunswick, NJ: Rutgers University Press, 1994), 21.

23 Debra Gimlin, *Body Work: Beauty and Self-Image in American Culture* (Berkeley: University of California Press, 2002).

24 Kim Toffoletti, *Cyborgs and Barbie Dolls: Feminism, Popular Culture and the Posthuman Body* (London and New York: Bloomsbury, 2007).

25 Laura Spielvogel, *Working Out in Japan: Shaping the Female Body in Tokyo Fitness Clubs* (Durham, NC: Duke University Press, 2003).

26 Famously, in medieval Japan, feminine beauty also included shaved and painted eyebrows and blackened teeth, along with a whitened face and small, red-painted lips.

27 Fima Lifshitz, *An African Journey through Its Art* (Bloomington, IN: AuthorHouse, 2009); Avner Shakarov and Lyubov Senatorova, *Traditional African Art: An Illustrated Study* (Jefferson, NC: McFarland, 2015).

28 http://www.state.gov/j/drl/rls/irf/2006/71342.htm.

29 Jun'ichi Isomae, *Religious Discourse in Modern Japan: Religion, State, and Shintō* (Boston, MA: Brill, 2014).

30 Peter Kornicki and James McMullen (Eds.), *Religion in Japan: Arrows to Heaven and Earth* (Cambridge: Cambridge University Press, 1996).

31 John Breen and Mark Teeuwen, *A New History of Shinto* (Hoboken, NJ: John Wiley & Sons, 2010).

32 Jennifer Oldstone-Moore, *Taoism: Origins, Beliefs, Practices, Holy Texts, Sacred Places* (New York: Oxford University Press, 2003).
33 Russell Kirkland, *Taoism: The Enduring Tradition* (Abingdon: Routledge, 2004).
34 Kenji Matsuo, *A History of Japanese Buddhism* (Folkestone: Global Oriental, 2007).
35 Miriam Kinsey, *Contemporary* Netsuke (Rutland, VT: Tuttle, 2013); Barbara Teri Okada, *Netsuke: Masterpieces from the Metropolitan Museum of Art* (New York: Metropolitan Museum of Art, 1982).
36 Ben-Ami Shillony, *The Jews and the Japanese: The Successful Outsiders* (Rutland, VT: Tuttle, 1992).
37 Constance McPhee and Nadine Orenstein, *Infinite Jest: Caricature and Satire from Leonardo to Levine* (New York: Metropolitan Museum of Art, 2011); Ralph Shikes, *The Indignant Eye: The Artist as Social Critic in Prints and Drawings from the 15th Century to Picasso* (New York: Beacon Press, 1969).
38 Ernest Gombrich, "The Principles of Caricature," *British Journal of Medical Psychology* 17 (1938): 319.
39 Abiola Irele and Biodun Jeyifo (Eds.), *The Oxford Encyclopedia of African Thought. Vol. 1: Abol-Impe* (Oxford: Oxford University Press, 2010); Ben-Ami Scharfstein, *Art without Borders: A Philosophical Exploration of Art and Humanity* (Chicago, IL: University of Chicago Press, 2009).
40 Molefi Kete Asante and Ama Mazama (Eds.), *Encyclopedia of African Religion (Vol. 1)* (Thousand Oaks, CA: Sage Publications, 2009).

References

Asante, Molefi Kete and Ama Mazama (Eds.). *Encyclopedia of African Religion (Vol. 1)*. Thousand Oaks, CA: Sage Publications, 2009.

Breen, John and Mark Teeuwen. *A New History of Shinto*. Hoboken, NJ: John Wiley & Sons, 2010.

Brown, Azby. *The Genius of Japanese Carpentry: Secrets of an Ancient Craft*. Rutland, VT: Tuttle, 2014.

Clancey, Gregory. "Modernity and Carpenters: Daiku Technique and Meiji Technocracy." In *Building a Modern Japan: Science, Technology and Medicine in the Meiji Era and Beyond*, edited by Morris Law, 183–206. New York: Palgrave Macmillan, 2005.

Cross, Nigel. *Designerly Ways of Knowing*. London: Springer, 2006.

Dima, Nicholas. *Culture, Religion, and Geopolitics*. United States of America: Xlibris Corporation, 2010.

Ditmar, Helga. *Consumer Culture, Identity and Well-Being: The Search for the "Good Life" and the "Body Perfect"*. Hove and New York: Psychology Press, 2007.

Eider, Shimon. *Halachos of Tefillin*. Jerusalem: Feldheim, 1984.

Fathy, Hassan. *Architecture for the Poor: An Experiment in Rural Egypt*. Chicago, IL: University of Chicago Press, 1973.

Gimlin, Debra. *Body Work: Beauty and Self-Image in American Culture*. Berkeley: University of California Press, 2002.

Gombrich, Ernest. "The Principles of Caricature." *British Journal of Medical Psychology* 17 (1938): 319–342.

Grogan, Sarah. *Body Image: Understanding Body Dissatisfaction in Men, Women and Children*. 4th ed. Abingdon: Routledge, 2021.

Hahner-Herzog, Iris, Maria Kecskesi and Lazlo Vajda. *African Masks: From the Barbier-Mueller Collection*. New York: Prestel, 2007.

Irele, Abiola and Biodun Jeyifo (Eds.). *The Oxford Encyclopedia of African Thought. Vol. 1: Abol-Impe*. Oxford: Oxford University Press, 2010.

Isomae, Jun'ichi. *Religious Discourse in Modern Japan: Religion, State, and Shintō*. Boston, MA: Brill, 2014.

Julier, Guy. "From Visual Culture to Design Culture." *Design Issues* 22, no. 1 (2006): 64–76.

Kinsey, Miriam. *Contemporary Netsuke*. Rutland, VT: Tuttle, 2013.

Kirkland, Russell. *Taoism: The Enduring Tradition*. Abingdon: Routledge, 2004.

Koizumi, Kazuko. *Traditional Japanese Furniture*. Tokyo: Kodansha international, 1986.

Kornicki, Peter and James McMullen (Eds.). *Religion in Japan: Arrows to Heaven and Earth*. Cambridge: Cambridge University Press, 1996.

Lifshitz, Fima. *An African Journey through Its Art*. Bloomington, IN: AuthorHouse, 2009.

Manzini, Ezio. "Design Culture and Dialogic Design." *Design Issues* 32, no. 1 (2016): 52–59.

Markakis, John. *Ethiopia: The Last Two Frontiers*. Vol. 10. Suffolk: Boydell & Brewer Ltd, 2011.

Matsuo, Kenji. *A History of Japanese Buddhism*. Folkestone: Global Oriental, 2007.

McPhee, Constance and Nadine Orenstein. *Infinite Jest: Caricature and Satire from Leonardo to Levine*. New York: Metropolitan Museum of Art, 2011.

Meadmore, Clement. *The Modern Chair: Classic Designs by Thonet, Breuer, Le Corbusier, Eames and Others*. Mineola, NY: Dover Publications, 2019.

Moors, Annelies. "Wearing Gold." In *Border Fetishisms: Material Objects in Unstable Spaces*, edited by Patricia Spyer, 208–223. Abingdon: Routledge, 1998.

Neiman, Moshe. *Tefillin: An Illustrated Guide to Their Makeup and Use*. Jerusalem: Feldheim, 1995.

Okada, Barbara Teri. *Netsuke: Masterpieces from the Metropolitan Museum of Art*. New York: Metropolitan Museum of Art, 1982.

O'Sickey, Ingebord Majer. "Barbie Magazine and the Aesthetic Commodification of Girls' Bodies." In *On Fashion*, edited by Shari Benstock and Suzanne Ferriss, 21–40. New Brunswick, NJ: Rutgers University Press, 1994.

Oldstone-Moore, Jennifer. *Taoism: Origins, Beliefs, Practices, Holy Texts, Sacred Places*. New York: Oxford University Press, 2003.

Pollock, Griselda. *Vision and Difference: Femininity, Feminism and the Histories of Art*. Abingdon: Routledge, 1988.

Pollock, Griselda. *Differencing the Canon: Feminism and the Writing of Art's Histories*. Abingdon: Routledge, 2013.

Postell, Jim. *Furniture Design*. London: John Wiley and Sons, 2012.

Raizman, David. *History of Modern Design: Graphics and Products since the Industrial Revolution*. London: Laurence King, 2003.

Russell, Rebecca Ross. *Gender and Jewelry: A Feminist Analysis*. Medford, MA: Tufts University, 2010.

Scharfstein, Ben-Ami. *Art without Borders: A Philosophical Exploration of Art and Humanity*. Chicago, IL: University of Chicago Press, 2009.

Shakarov, Avner and Senatorova, Lyubov. *Traditional African Art: An Illustrated Study.* Jefferson, NC: McFarland, 2015.

Shikes, Ralph. *The Indignant Eye: The Artist as Social Critic in Prints and Drawings from the 15th Century to Picasso.* New York: Beacon Press, 1969.

Shillony, Ben-Ami. *The Jews and the Japanese: The Successful Outsiders.* Rutland, VT: Tuttle, 1992.

Spielvogel, Laura. *Working Out in Japan: Shaping the Female Body in Tokyo Fitness Clubs.* Durham, NC: Duke University Press, 2003.

Toffoletti, Kim. *Cyborgs and Barbie Dolls: Feminism, Popular Culture and the Posthuman Body.* London and New York: Bloomsbury, 2007.

Vogel, Susan (Ed.). *For Spirits and Kings: African Art from the Paul and Ruth Tishman Collection.* New York: Metropolitan Museum of Art, 1981.

Wolf, Naomi. *The Beauty Myth: How Images of Beauty Are Used against Women.* New York: HarperCollins, 2002.

4 Sensory Type

From Motivation to Activation

Minjee Jeon

Introduction

The introductory focus of this work is to cultivate students' DEI-centric motivations by examining humanistic values and socially conscious initiatives. The resulting DEI statements from this process are then visually manifested through collaborative efforts and brought to life through the creative use of graphic media. This involves further exploration of innovative tools and methodologies that examine the functions, concepts, and perceptions of digital media, leading to immersive experiences and meaningful dialogues. Through a multi-layered approach, the work aims to equip students with a flexible and open mindset to design diverse and innovative audio-visual communications that can tackle a range of challenges, including sociocultural and technological issues.

Design Pedagogy

Preparing for the Future

Pedagogy is vital for students as members of society, as it equips them with the knowledge, skills, and attitudes necessary to be active, informed, and responsible citizens. Design pedagogy (Escobar 2018; Thackara 2004), particularly in the context of graphic design, can further "advocate for new kinds of engagement between design and the world."[1] Through design thinking, design educational strategies enable students to live more meaningful and sociocultural responsible lives.[2] This creates a diverse creative process in which research discovers new areas of design that connect vision and reality (Laurel 2003). Diversity, Equity, and Inclusion (DEI) in design thinking, for instance, can bring about an intersection between social humanities and design that lays the groundwork for students to commit to and contribute to society by harnessing the power of visual communication design. This design pedagogy also incorporates up-to-date education and creative practice derived from a framework that prioritizes the evolving needs and perspectives of users

DOI: 10.4324/9781032616650-4

and communities, as well as the needs of the times, in response to trends and technologies.[3] Through this creative education, students develop their critical thinking skills so they can engage with different perspectives and cultures and think about ways to serve their respective communities. Therefore, design education today holds a great responsibility in preparing students for the future by helping them find their place in the world and empowering them to create designs that can have a positive impact on society.

MSU Graphic Design Mission and Challenges

The Graphic Design programme at Montana State University (MSU) is dedicated to preparing students to take a leading role in contemporary design practices. The curriculum is designed to create a student-centred learning environment that encourages ongoing personal development through integrated learning, discovery, and engagement. The programme achieves this through a range of activities, such as creative problem-solving, research, case studies, design thinking, and collaboration.

Problem-solving is an important aspect of graphic design, but today's students are faced with complex design problems. In her work, *Complex Problems*, Professor Meredith Davis defines these problems as "wicked, poorly defined, and ever-expanding in scope," and says that a linear approach to dealing with one component or element at a time is not suitable for today's dynamic conditions.[4] For example, in the continuously evolving and complex digital realm, design not only requires constant change but also considers its impact on all aspects of daily life that depend on digital technology and information and communication technology (Escobar 2018, 41). While the social and cultural complexities of our lives are also impacted by these evolving issues, MSU students face the additional challenge of being nimble in responding to these sociocultural issues due to Montana's geographic isolation and culturally constrained diverse environment. (According to the 2020 Montana Census, whites aggregate 88.7% of the population, Black or African American alone sum up 0.6%, and American Indians and Alaska Natives alone make up 6.6%.[5] Additionally, in MSU Graphic Design programme in Spring 2021, more than 96% of students were white.[6])

So how can design education contribute to designing and shaping the world and our lives? Successful complex problems solution requires creative insight in both planning and analysis and working as a team to bridge various disciplines (Davis 2018b, 2). Additionally, for design education to make a difference (Willis 2015), it must include introductions and discourses on social structures and social change.[7] Further, the key question is to ask what are the design strategies that enable humans to lead more meaningful and responsible lives in a complex world (Thackara 2004). These questions suggest the direction of design education that can be thought of in response to the complexities and issues of various regions, societies, cultures, and technologies.

The Power and Engagement of Digital Visual Communication Design

At the height of the pandemic, the United States was experiencing a period of surge in racial inequality driven by police violence and conflict against Black people fighting for their rights. These movements were vividly expressed through text and visual messages on digital platforms and social media, amplifying the voices of marginalized communities and groups advocating for them. Ubiquitous hashtags and the silent protest of unison black screen posts were some examples of how collective voices were manifested.

Digital products cannot function outside of a social context, as digital products live and transform the social world (Kommonen 2013). Therefore, "doing digital design also means designing society, and designers ought to take a stand as a driver of social change."[8] As shown in these movements, the strength of digital visual communication lies in raising issues and expanding the dialogue. Similarly, despite the lack of exposure to racial diversity and culture in Montana, digital media and its communication have allowed students to identify and engage with the current sociopolitical environment. Considering the function of digital media and platforms as a place where individual communication and collective voices are expressed and heard as a transcendent place, it is a sociocultural point of view where the importance of digital communication using text and images is highlighted.

According to Kari-Hans Kommonen, a theorist at Aalto University Media Lab, "In addition to computers, software, digital information, and media, the materials of digital design also include communities, processes, practices, and culture, and designers need to be equipped with the right skill to deal with these elements."[9] Applied pedagogically, graphic design students who study visual communication as a means of dialogue can demonstrate the ability of design to contribute to the community as a meaningful experience.

Thus, from the complex issues and challenges to the capabilities and hopes of digital design, it has inspired the following design pedagogy to guide students to develop socially conscious design initiatives that cultivate a sound understanding of sustainable visual communication systems.

Project "Sensory Type: From Motivation to Activation"

The project *Sensory Type: From Motivation to Activation* arose from approaching and responding to complex issues of society, culture, and technology and embodying how design can advance creative studio practices. Emphasis is placed on research to bridge theories and design frameworks to create practices that "question the role of digital technologies in transforming a place, experience and design context."[10] In addition to DEI in design thinking, the work prepares students for designing innovative communication systems and experiences that increase social awareness in the Montana community and among MSU graphic design students.

The project is divided into two phases: Motivation and Activation. The first Motivation phase builds and reinforces the motivation that leads students not only to examine sociocultural issues but also to ideate methods for "designing together" according to the theme of DEI. Teamwork emerges through DEI-centric design thinking methods and research.

In the second Activation phase, students implement creative technical methods to activate tools and dialogue through artistic production. Continuing their DEI-centric design practice, students are guided to transform socially conscious design initiatives into visual communication as a means of dialogue and design experiences that serve the community.

Sensory Type is a project that originated from a problem identified in the state of Montana but the application of the DEI in Design framework aspires to bridge engagement with the community by using it flexibly in various design tasks and fields.

This project aims to achieve the following:

1 Conduct creative research that aligns with the commitment of higher education, including MSU, to support the diversity mission while emphasizing the importance of DEI-centric (Diversity, Equity, and Inclusion) design practices.[11]
2 Develop socially conscious design initiatives that promote emotional intelligence, personal commitment, cognitive flexibility, and collaborative practices, and prioritize equity and inclusion in design.
3 Demonstrate an understanding of the vital role of design in promoting healthy societies through creative and critical research, artistic production, and design solutions that address social issues.
4 Foster an inclusive learning environment that emphasizes teamwork and independence, encouraging students to approach problems through DEI in design thinking.
5 Provide learning opportunities for students and communities to engage in design-driven social change that promotes sustainable, equitable, and inclusive dialogue.

Motivation

Building Motivation through Exploration of Humanistic Values

The Motivation phase examines the social and cultural issues centring on human interests and values. It initiates research to build students' motivation and commitment to discussing why and how we can create a sustainable dialogue around issues of DEI.

Ethical and humanistic values are common human values that create emotional connections and bonds between people. Core values also act as indicators of business management in modern global society, instilling trust and providing positive experiences by meeting the demands and standards of public responsibility. Professor Davis states in *Core Values Matter* that "audiences evaluate organizations based on the consistency between their messages and the values expressed in their products, services and/or social behaviour." When all the pillars of business operations are guided by ethical and humanistic values, these premises enable employees to be more productive, customers to be more loyal, and businesses to build strong relationships with people, including local communities, to better prepare for the future (Davis 2018; Cohen and Warwick 2008). Businesses and organizations increasingly practice creating an ethos consistent with the values of social equity and inclusion.[12] These business trends and practices help designers shape decisions and strategies that guide people's behaviours and attitudes through design based on humanistic values.[13]

Applying this from an educational point of view, the first phase of Motivation sets the design initiative with students' beliefs and values as the starting point of the work. Studio practices and design works that are oriented towards what students believe in and value not only improve their individual capabilities and interests but also enhance overall studio attitude by learning about the importance of common benefits of collaboration. DEI in design thinking are based on shared human interests and values that drive DEI-centric practices, which enable students to create meaningful work that shapes the attitudes and behaviours of their target audiences. Throughout their work, students demonstrated that they prioritized groups and communities that could benefit from and actively participate in their design work and endeavours. As such, design education that instils a belief that one's work can make a positive difference in the community does more than create "design for good" (2) or "socially good design" for students, which, in turn, makes students more motivated and invested in their work.[14] Through the idea of change by design (Brown 2009), this design thinking enables both individuals and teams to generate ground-breaking ideas that are implemented and impacted using an accessible and holistic approach to innovation.[15]

With motives reinforced to work towards a sustainable DEI in design, students ideate methods to "designing together" that align with the practice of DEI in design. In this DEI-driven design, Sensory Type not only establishes the need for teamwork and collaboration but also lays the groundwork for sustainability only through collaboration.

Therefore, with the importance of teamwork, a total of four groups are presented in this work and each group consists of four members. Each group of students discusses the core values and selects common themes related to DEI. Each student first approaches a problem from an individual perspective and then reflects as a group to obtain and converge different perspectives. With this, students next embark on writing a DEI statement that reflects their motivation and commitment to addressing sociocultural issues.

Creating DEI Statement

Creating a DEI statement that reflects value-driven motivations and socially conscious initiatives is not just verbal articulation. As Sherry Hakimi puts it in a Fast Company article (2015), "An organization without purpose manages people and resources,[16] while an organization with purpose mobilizes people and resources," a purpose and clear narrative help and guide all activities. Narratives, or verbal expressions, not only govern our thoughts, beliefs, and actions, but to a greater extent, they shape our social culture. When the words of belief and thought become the purpose, they become a driving force that motivates people to act. With these premises, enabling sustainable discourse and creative activity both inside and outside the classroom that serves the community is the goal leading students to make DEI statements. Here examining our core values and raising questions about our sociocultural status through the DEI statement provides concrete direction for the project's initiatives. This will inspire the way students engage creatively with their communities, further strengthening their motivation and commitment to working towards a more equitable and inclusive society.

The student groups writing the DEI statement are facilitated by the theoretical framework of the following:

1   Study the role and importance of transition design.
2   Strengthening teamwork through DEI in design thinking.
3   Access complex issues through a problem-framing approach.

Transition Design

> Transition Design acknowledges that we are living in 'transition times' and takes as its central premise the need for societal transitions to more sustainable futures and the belief that design has a role to play in these transitions.[17]
>
> –Carnegie Mellon University Mission statement

Without an understanding of social structures and the adoption of change, design education cannot contribute to a genuine change (Willis 2015). The transition design framework frames design discourse and education that mediates through design in adapting to the growing social challenges of today's world. Transition design, which seems to be close to humanities due to the application of social theory to the field of design (72), induces new design methods based on the theory of change,[18] open mindset and attitude, mindfulness, and willingness to collaborate (Irwin 2015).[19] This new method emphasizes designers as facilitators and mediators rather than experts and creates spaces for collaboration and engagement through design (Escobar 2018, 33). Design research and practice as "an attempt to build an alternative cultural vision as a driver of social change" (34) in Sensory Type, we aim to expand the impact of design on local and global communities. In this sense, design is seen not as changing the world, but as part of changing the world itself, as an agent of social change (Gatt and Ingold 2013, 146).

While its mission is vast, taking designers' own mindsets and stances as an integral part of the design process (Irwin, Kossoff, and Tonkinwise 2015, 3) gives student designers a sense of agency to envision larger goals. Building on what Gatt and Ingold say, "we have to make the future for ourselves, but that can only be done through dialogue," student designers can go further and tackle existing problems and imagine new possibilities based on creating a dialogue about "human life itself."[20] Based on designers' mindsets, attitudes, and their dialogue, transition design champions place-based networked solutions and pursues projects that enrich our understanding of our life and ourselves.[21]

Carnegie Mellon University puts forward the role of transition design in transforming society (Source: Escobar 2018, 153): (1) Developing compelling narratives and visions of the future, based on the preconception of lifestyles as human-scaled, place-based, and globally connected in terms of technology, information, and culture. (2) Amplifying and connecting the grassroots efforts of local communities. (3) Participating in transdisciplinary teams to develop innovative, place-based solutions for the transition to more sustainable futures. The framework suggests an empirical model of teamwork and discussion, leading to a design approach that is oriented towards a long-term, sustainable vision of the future. Creating "visions" of and for change is a key approach to focus on a methodology that facilitates discussion rather than a fully developed strategy (Escobar 2018; Irwin, Kossoff, and Tonkinwise 2015).[22]

Drawing inspiration from these frameworks, the Sensory Type emphasizes the importance of considering social issues in design, with a focus on creating more inclusive design processes and outcomes that consider the experiences of people from diverse backgrounds. At this stage of writing the DEI statement, students in each group apply the following framework to seek discussion and design for a long-term and sustainable dialogue:

1 Put marginalized voices at the centre: Actively seek out and integrate the perspectives and experiences of underrepresented groups and voices to better understand their unique needs and challenges.
2 Collaboration across design disciplines and methodologies: Facilitate effective and equitable communication between team members using a variety of design methods and disciplines. For example, students envision creative communication systems to improve collaboration and sustainability in projects.
3 Envision long-term change: Develop sustainable solutions with ongoing community feedback on the design process. This feedback loop will help design solutions to address relevant societal challenges facing our world today.

Committed to an inclusive gesture that considers equity and encourages diversity of thought, DEI in design thinking provides the next avenue for that practice.

Diversity, Equity, and Inclusion in Design Thinking

> Being a transition designer means adopting different values and perspectives. It is therefore a process of learning, but, for the same reason, a challenge.[23]
>
> –Cameron Tonkinwise, "Design's (Dis)Orders and Transition Design"

In today's complex environment, DEI in design thinking and practice help design students to be responsive to sociocultural issues, as well as to reach a wider audience by creating diverse, inclusive, and equitable gestures that communicate DEI-based messages.

Diversity is essential to creative education because the lack of diversity makes it more difficult for creative people to explore ingenious solutions from different perspectives. Achieving racial diversity in the MSU design programmes can be challenging if diversity is understood only as representing all groups involved in race. In addition to including factors such as background, ability/disability, and gender, the concept of diversity can be extended to include a wider range of people through a creative lens. Diversity in design, or "diversity of thought,"[24] is seeing things differently, and this perspective values incorporating diverse "experiences, perspectives, and creativity" in design (Carroll 2014). Thus, encouraging diversity in design education, discourse, and practice, extends the relevance of design in all spheres of society by promoting role models, opportunities, and public awareness in the face of indifference, insensitivity, and outright discrimination (2–3). When identifying sociocultural issues in the DEI, students on each team seek to explore the issue from as many different angles and perspectives as possible.

While equality is defined as access to opportunity, equity is more than opportunity and thinks about the barriers that create unequal access to opportunities (Gaspar and Ogbu 2015). Equity in design thinking generates discussions that orient co-creation and decision-making towards equality of opportunity. As an exercise for equity design thinking, students work together to find a way for all team members to participate in an equitable solution.

Finally, reflecting on all preceding practices invites inclusive gestures in which the practice of inclusion in design thinking "reflects the opinions of audiences for design and finds ways to listen to many voices" (Miller 2017). The AIGA Diversity & Inclusion Task Force also considers inclusive thinking to activate critical thinking, saying: "When thinking is inclusive, it enhances creativity and the ability to generate more ideas and better solutions—which, in turn, activates the ability to be innovative."[25] As the DEI in design envisions extending the conversation to the community, an inclusive approach allows all students and communities to build a strong foundation for success.

Collectively, DEI in design thinking sparks discussion on DEI-related issues that need to be addressed by DEI-centric practice and opens a diverse and inclusive space for sustainable dialogue. By enabling students to identify themselves as independent and diverse role models, and contributing to developing multiple perspectives, students leverage DEI discourse in design to develop their ability to connect design in all spheres of society.

Problem-Framing

In today's expanding information and technology experience, the envisioning of new communication models acknowledges that "problem components are interdependent and in a constantly changing relationship."[26] Interrelated and complex problem structures in various domains of society, culture, and technology lead to questions about how they affect creative practice and design education. As mentioned earlier, problem-solving is an important aspect of graphic design, but problems that require more than an individual's abilities and skills should shift the focus of the problem. Given the scale and complexity of contemporary sociocultural and technical issues, "problem-framing" allows design students to get to the root of the problem and ask critical questions. Through questions, it gives meaning to designs that focus on human experience and context.[27] As problem-framing activates problem-related questions, the conceptualization of this process reveals values within a group of students and provides a clear sense of aligned goals. Therefore, rather than an idealized, impractical solution, this approach provides a new framework that generates ideas for how to communicate a problem.

Problem identification and problem-framing in design go beyond problem-solving and aim for ethics that have fostered sensibility that contributes to creating a better world (Antonelli 2014). Problem-framing is also about giving direction, such as an open ending rather than a closure with a solution. An approach like this is thus "critical, active, and organic," using design as a medium to serve society.[28] When students understand the nature of the problem, it creates opportunities to arrive at insightful dialogue that fosters innovation and change. It is important to work towards reaching a better discussion rather than drawing conclusions from the question itself or expecting an effect.

In summary, the Motivation phase emphasizes the development of active dialogue based on DEI-centric design thinking to foster personal commitment and emotional intelligence with strong humanistic value-driven motivation. As value-centred work is both the seed and the engine of change, it motivates students by providing them with goals and direction to move forward. To ultimately arrive at the DEI statement, this phase is layered in a step-by-step approach. Through integrating transition design thinking, DEI in design thinking process, and the problem-framing approach, the Sensory Type in Motivation phase promotes a discussion of possible and desirable communities and societies.

As a new generation of designers comes together to envision design as a long-term, sustainable dialogue, students are shaped to become informed, responsible, and engaged members of society ready to make meaningful contributions to their communities and the world at large. With a strong commitment and motives to DEI-centred research and value-driven narratives, the next phase of the project focuses on the artistic side of design production and activation.

Activation

In the Activation phase, students visually communicate the messages from the narratives and DEI statements they developed in the previous Motivation phase. The phase leads to ideation and the creative-making process guided by the concepts of "activation of design" and "activation of dialogue." The project Sensory Type continues to focus on the themes of DEI, while advancing and putting them into action through hands-on collaborative work and artistic production. Considering the contemporary technological environment and tools as influencing factors in graphic design communication, the studio leads student groups to expand traditional design methods and transform them to create innovative and inspiring spaces for dialogue. Through production, students aim to explore and create a more diverse and inclusive approach to visually presenting messages using graphic techniques and visual communication methods.

Expanding the Discourse of Motion Graphics

The project Sensory Type is conducted in the Motion Graphics class, one of the technology-focused courses within the MSU Graphic Design programme. The course equips students with time-based media and computational applications to succeed in the digital realm, creating compelling animated works for use in digital messaging campaigns, public engagement, and message exchange. Motion graphics is an effective tool for reaching large audiences through various social media platforms. The design pedagogy in this course emphasizes the role of time-based design in influencing social culture and inspiring and transforming feelings and ideas through audio-visual motion.

The MSU graphic design curriculum provides instruction in both digital and physical processes, teaching the principles of graphic design through hands-on disciplines such as crafting, letterpress, and laser cutting techniques. As an extension of the curriculum, in the work of Sensory Type, students in the Motion Graphics course not only utilize animation and motion technology but also connect various tools to create meaningful experiences that prepare them for new communication skills. By combining the teaching of modern digital technologies with traditional hands-on skills, students can develop an integration of prototyping techniques leading to unpredictable design solutions and creative thinking skills.

Design Process: Activation of Design Tools

The production of the Sensory Type project involves four elements and methods: typography, three-dimensional physical elements, motion graphics, and projection mapping. Students learn about the strengths of each medium and how to synthesize them to create an installation design that enables audiences to experience the DEI messages in an engaging way.

1 Manifesting messages through typography

Typography is fundamental to graphic design and enables students to exercise their perceptual and conceptual skills in visual communication. Typography has many uses, from making words legible to evoking emotion and bringing them to life.[29] It is a medium and methodology to spark ideas, as it is not only an effective way to convey a message but also serves to grab the viewer's attention by mimicking the tone of a word or sentence.[30]

Based on this knowledge, students convert the DEI statements developed in the Motivation phase into typographic designs. That is, turning the written words into an appropriate and meaningful visual form of typography. Students can use existing typefaces and fonts or create their own typefaces by modifying existing type designs to give them new looks. Students explore the typographical relationship between form and content, considering the communicative nature of emotions and experiences that go beyond surface-level reading.

2 Manual fabrication of large-scale physical 3D structures

Next, the DEI statement expressed in digital typography design is converted into physical form. Students engage in group work to create large-scale three-dimensional typographic structures, either by hand or using digital laser cutting methods (Figures 4.1 and 4.2). These sculptural forms are composed of letters, words, and shapes derived from their statements. They are also painted white to give the impression of an unfinished (inactive) appearance. While the form is still legible and readable on the surface, the space of the large white pieces serves as the canvas area for the next step in projection mapping.

3 Time-based media and motion graphics design

If the sculptural figure of a DEI statement is a condensed form of a message that exists in physical space, in this step students use the properties of time-based media to overcome the limitations of physical properties. Using motion graphics techniques and the audio-visual elements of animation, students expand the DEI message to convey the full narrative through kinetic-type animation and refine the aesthetic elements of movement and timing to appeal aptly to the human senses.[31] Kinetic type is when the type meets movement through animation techniques that can enhance the communication of the text. In addition to the formal quality of typography, time-based motion design, and its artistic elements in kinetic type can set a mood and either explicitly direct or manipulate the viewer's attention through wordplay. The synthesis of attention to timing, sound, and graphics makes it more powerful, effective, and engaging than stills. The combination of auditory elements and visual representations provides sharp sensory stimulation to

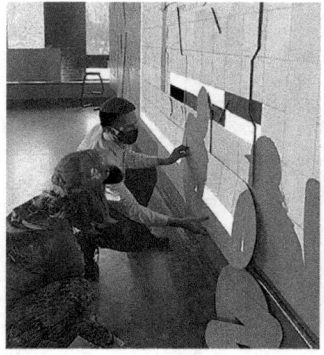

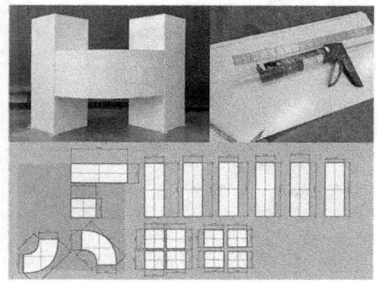

Figure 4.1 A group of students assembling the 3D Sensory Type. 2021. Photo: Minjee Jeon.

Figure 4.2 Student group's 3D Sensory Type prototyping process. 2021. Photo: Lauren Baca.

enhance the communication of ideas, emotions, and messages. These motion graphics and animations are used as elements of projection mapping over the sculpture pieces of the DEI statement. So, when the projection map is turned on, i.e., "activated," it fully projects the message with rich emotional delivery.

4 Bridging physical and digital: immersive installations with projection mapping

Projection mapping is the pinnacle of technology that uses lights and images to map the projection of light onto an object, building, or person.

So far, students have transformed their DEI statements into physical sculptures and digital animations. In this final step, the students then projection-map their animations onto their large-scale 3D structures, activating the inactive messages in a dynamic way, as if bringing an inanimate object to life. As an installation form, the projection mapping technique transforms ordinary surfaces into dynamic, animated works of art, providing viewers with the opportunity for an impactful experience to share lasting sensory memories. Additionally, in the next step of preparing a proposal for an immersive installation in a public space, students are given ample space to display their impactful message, extending the audience to the public outside the classroom. Throughout this process, students experience the transformation of the medium into a readable, imaginative, and inclusive space that fosters reflection and discussion (Figure 4.3).

Activation of DEI in Design

In the project Sensory Type, students worked together to conduct research, brainstorm messages, and visualize the DEI statements and narrative as an

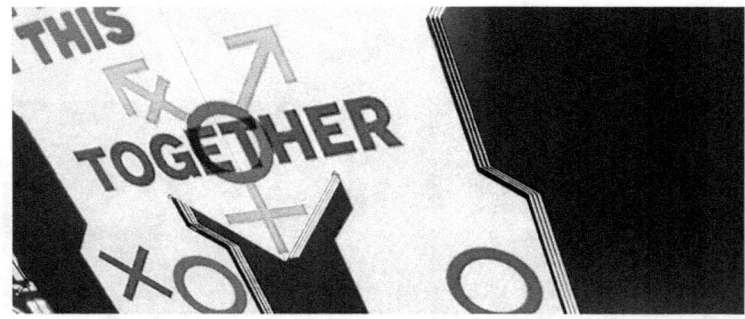

Figure 4.3 Hubbell, James. "M/On" (parts from the group TEAM), 2021. Video projection, mixed media, surround sound. Dimensions variable. Duration: 30 sec. Photo: James Hubbell.

experiential space. By working upwards from the root of the problem, they recognized that the components of the problem are constantly changing as well as interdependently affecting each other. This kind of group project is uncommon in graphic design programmes, especially for motion graphic design work, so it was valuable for promoting group cooperation and introducing DEI in Design practice. In addition to design constraints and established rules, students were expected to devise a design solution that reflected DEI practices within their groups. How could collaborative group work create inclusive and equitable design solutions that reflected diverse perspectives?

This project includes a total of four groups (Okay, Team, Life, and Montana), with four students in each group. Students were assigned to groups to conduct research, set the tone for socially conscious DEI initiatives, and brainstorm messages outlining the DEI narrative. Each student's individual designs had to function independently as well as in groups. The success of group work depended on strengthening each student's message through collaboration and creating new meaning.

An example, one of the student group works is detailed below to demonstrate how students independently and collaboratively engaged in the DEI in design thinking process to arrive at the final production (Figure 4.4).

Student Group 1, "okay"

The DEI Statement and Their DEI in Design Thinking

This group discusses the subconscious and insidious sexism that exists in the K-12 school system that creates an insufficient foundation for female self-esteem. The group chose the word "okay" to represent the passive, submissive responses that teachers often provide in response to a girl's question or comment, an issue identified in Myra and David Sadker's essay "Missing in Interaction." These acceptance responses, like okay, may have good

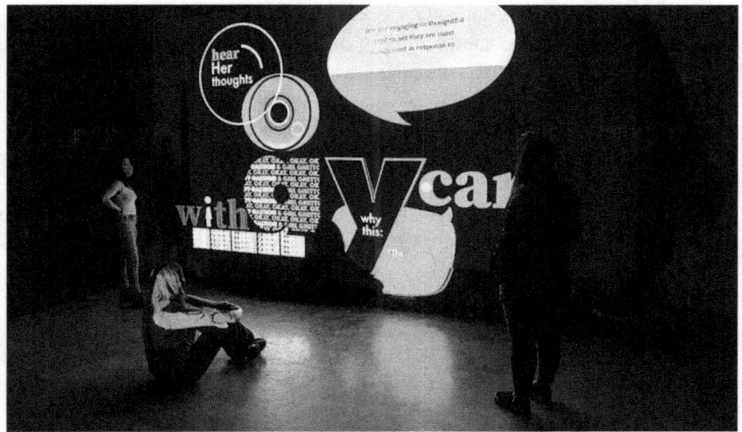

Figure 4.4 Group "okay." "Sensory Type–okay," 2021. Video projection, mixed media, surround sound. Dimensions variable. Duration: 30 sec. Photo: Nicholas Manship.

intentions, but lack constructive value. When girls don't get feedback on how to move forward, they become less engaged in the classroom and feel overwhelmed by their male peers.

To visually express the constructive value of this word in a neutral tone, the group chose the typeface, Futura Extra-Bold. They also decided to use lowercase letters to reduce visual weight and reflect how little a word is worth. The four group members each assigned the four letters of "okay" as an equitable and inclusive solution to the workload and spatial domains, where different and diverse ideas, perspectives, and opinions on the framing issues can be reflected and play a role. The division of space and work allowed each student to creatively interact with their assigned character, reflecting individual statements, messages, thoughts, and feelings through graphics and kinetic animation. Nonetheless, as a unified whole, the students created an impactful delivery through coherence, considering the style and the tone of the message.

Student "o" highlights the shape of the letter "o," using rippled lines and circular spheres of text to create an animation that draws attention to the need to actively listen to young girls and hear their thoughts in K-12 education. Through the animation, the student aimed to point out the importance of providing constructive feedback to the girls rather than an unhelpful and passive "okay" response. While conveying the idea that rippling sound waves affect one source to another, the repetition of the text is intended to overwhelm the viewer with how the girls will feel at the teacher's passive response.

Student "k" generates the message "K quiets" driven by the phrase "Okay: It Quiets with Care" which is meant to convey that teachers care about their students, but a lack of enthusiasm will make students less engaged in their K-12

classes over time. Adding the cute speech bubble shape is an intuitive conceptualization of the sugar-coated rendition of the word "okay" to avoid conflict,
especially with a young female student. The animation from "K quiets" ironi-
cally expresses that those passive and unenthusiastic responses in the classroom
are all too common for girls and should be addressed with active interest.

Student "a" focused on the teacher's interaction influencing the social
interactions of girls and boys on the playground as a conceptual narrative.
The phrase "Boy Bastion & Girl Ghetto" in the letter "a" referred to an article
the group read on the topic, highlighting how boys segregate themselves from
girls because teachers make the girls seem like subspecies. "OKAY" and "&
Girl Ghetto" were not visible at first because boys are given more attention
in the classroom. The student added the word "girl," and in the selected font,
the letter "i" in the word "girl" gave the impression of a girl. Through animation, the rest of the letters were forcibly separated from the girl-shaped child,
emphasizing the sense of alienation.

Student "y" (Figure 4.5) uses radiating circles in the design to represent the
impact of a teacher's language and voice in a sexist system. The composition
offered an alternative way for teachers to interact with female students while
focusing on the math assignment rather than the female students' outfits.

Group Reflection

Our DEI statements in the installation identify the exclusion of female
students by teachers in grades K-12. In seeking to inform aspiring educators on and off campus at MSU, our group constructed an immersive
projection mapping installation to raise awareness of how the "okay"
classroom is anything but that. …This design was a great investigation
of working with multiple people to create a cohesive animation while
acknowledging every group member's individual style. The group's
compositions work very successfully both as individuals and as a whole,
therefore, each composition can easily standalone individually without
losing its effectiveness. Working as a group to edit a formally successful
composition from the illustrators representing the content within, we were
able to create agreed-upon boundaries for the design. These boundaries
allowed us to create animations with stylistic and conceptually grounded
places. …The success of the installation seems to lie in consistent engagement, gathering as many diverse perspectives as possible, and considering
an equitable and inclusive approach to facilitate the answering of our problems and questions. As we began to lean towards diverse individuation, the
project started to come to life. It showcased a diversity of thought that mirrors the diversity we all hope to see in student bodies and all institutions.
The DEI-centric thinking and the theme unites them and allows viewers
to examine the relationship between text, context, and our world. …We
believe that through DEI-based discussions, our group has successfully

moved one step closer to a construct that raises questions and leads to dialogue about a future that respects dynamics in youth, higher institutions, and communities. As a group, we are proud of what we have achieved while highlighting these big issues and each point we have taken in animation (Figure 4.6).

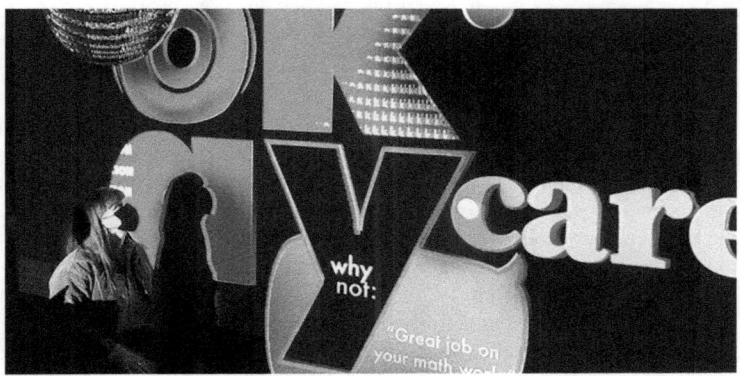

Figure 4.5 Budeski, Sarah. "Sensory Type–okay, portion 'y'," 2021. Video projection, mixed media, surround sound. Dimensions variable. Duration: 30 sec. Photo: Nicholas Manship.

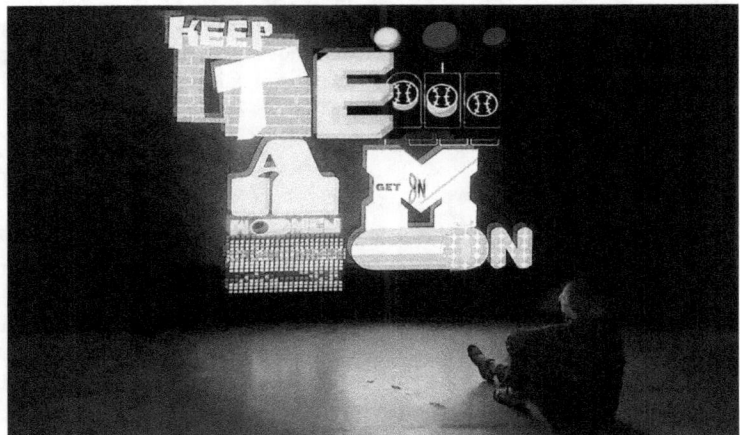

Figure 4.6 Group "team." "Sensory Type–TEAM," 2021. Video projection, mixed media, surround sound. Dimensions variable. Duration: 30 sec. Photo: Elle Olsztyn.

Activation of Messages, Active Reading

The contrast between projection-inactive and projection-active messages is compelling in terms of dynamic aesthetics and generating experience. As powerful as time-based media design is particularly in creating an immersive experience, graphic design education must drive continued expansion in today's digital media environment. Despite the complex nature of time-based media, which makes collaboration difficult, the DEI in design thinking has led to overcoming the complex design systems by guiding the creative integration of collaborative thinking. Students' Sensory Types thus successfully develop different ideas, messages, and designs that reflect each student's individuality while revealing the unity of each group's theme nurtured by the design system. Through motion graphics, students encounter opportunities to deconstruct, reconstruct, develop, and diversify the meaning of time-based visual communication design. This further led students to creatively combine and reshape elements of physical and digital typography to explore the syntax and pragmatics of words and sentences to make the delivery of communication more meaningful.

While the physical form of a typographic piece may initially suggest a surface-level message, the activation of projection map technology together with audio-visual animations thus reveals profound, insightful, and complex meanings. This intriguing relationship between physical typographic forms and projected kinetic animation liberates traditional reading, enabling designs that create multiple access points and providing insight into the creative reconstruction of a subject. These creative endeavours not only facilitate the creation of new forms and meanings that go beyond the traditional view of a problem but also encourage the audience to shift from passive viewing to active reading. Hereby synthesizing multimedia and examining the functions, concepts, and perceptions of digital media leads students to create stunning works that amplify the sensory experience of their audience through vivid and dynamic audio-visual communication systems.

Conclusion

The process of raising humanistic values through DEI in design leads to discussing new means and methods of communication design. It is a design approach to sociocultural contexts that can oscillate between "action and reflection" (Ehn, Nilsson, and Topgaard 2014).[32] In this way, the design production of the Sensory Type from matured "motivation to action (activation)" creates a unique collaboration that lays the groundwork for students to critically ask and answer questions about "who we are, how we create, and who we are creating for?"[33] There, students develop emotional intelligence, personal commitment, and cognitive flexibility for diverse, equitable, and inclusive collaborative practices that enable socially conscious design. As a result, Sensory Type presents a conceptual and experiential space that builds awareness of design-driven social change. When students take a leading role in design through DEI-focused communication strategies and studio practice, they gain confidence in applying and operating various visual communication systems. These skills and learning provide a foundation for students to respond flexibly and reflect on a range of technological, social, and cultural challenges.

In a media culture overflowing with messages of power and control, design education must foster visual literacy and critical thinking, and provide a way to respond in an ethical, humanistic, and sustainable dialogue through audio-visual communication design. The close relationship between our lives and design does not stop at improving the aesthetic and qualitative aspects of our surroundings but also creates change by mediating problems, disorders, and conflicts. Thus, DEI in design pedagogy in Sensory Type is not merely a means of expression or solving social and cultural problems.[34] With a core understanding that the world is a sum of diversity, the work brings students together to create meaningful work that focuses on creative methodologies to derive and integrate multiple perspectives. It drives the development of students' perceptual and conceptual skills by creating links to understanding different values through discourse on design and creative discipline.

Moving Forward

The project Sensory Type focuses on making a difference through student learning and research, community engagement, and outreach. As the project conducts creative research that emulates MSU's efforts to support diversity and build socially conscious initiatives, the work provides learning opportunities for students and communities across Montana to engage in design-driven social change. The work has been installed in public spaces, including local galleries, downtown, health centres, high schools, and more. As the work aims for design-driven social change through student and community engagement, the installation space has been transformed into a space for sustainable, equitable, and inclusive dialogue. Since the first launch of the project, the work has evolved through community-based initiatives and feedback. Moving forward, the next step for Sensory Type will be gathering reviews from community engagement to generate new metrics to measure impact and update strategies for ongoing work.

The Sensory Type will continue to envision forward-looking audio-visual communication designs that seek new ways of engagement between different students, disciplines, communities, and society. The DEI-centric pedagogical endeavour will hold students accountable for their role in shaping and communicating new ideas about inclusive spaces that inspire sustainable and humanistic dialogue. When DEI-centric design education can teach students the role and impact of responsible and socially conscious design, today's students will become tomorrow's teachers, and these young designers will teach us how to see the world and imagine a better future.

Notes

1 Arturo Escobar, *Designs for the Pluriverse Radical Interdependence, Autonomy, and the Making of Worlds* (Durham, NC and London: Duke University Press, 2018), 24.
2 John Thackara, *In the Bubble: Designing in a Complex World.* (Cambridge, MA: MIT Press, 2004).
3 Brenda Laurel, *Design Research: Methods and Perspectives.* (Cambridge, MA: MIT Press, ed. 2003).
4 Meredith Davis, "Complex Problems," *AIGA Design Futures Trend*, no. 1 (2018): 2.
5 Census.gov, "Montana Population Topped the 1 Million Mark in 2020," November 10, 2022, https://www.census.gov/content/census/en/library/stories/state-by-state/montana-population-change-between-census-decade.html/.
6 Minjee Jeon, "Montana State Graphic Design Student Survey–Spring Semester 2020," May 1, 2020.
7 Anne-Marie Willis, "Transition Design: The Need to Refuse Discipline and Transcend Instrumentalism," *Design Philosophy Papers* 13, no. 1 (2015): 72–73.
8 Kari-Hans Kommonen, "Design Ecosystems and the Design of Everyday Life." Unpublished paper, Arki Group, Media Lab, Aalto University, Helsinki (2013): 2.
9 Kommonen, "Design Ecosystems and the Design of Everyday Life," 1–2.
10 Escobar, *Designs for the Pluriverse*, 27.
11 "Diversity & Inclusion Framework Report - Office of the Provost | Montana State University" (n.d.). Diversity & Inclusion Framework Report - Office of the Provost | Montana State University, accessed June 5, 2019, https://www.montana.edu/provost/d_i.html.
12 Ben Cohen and Mai Warwick, *Values-Driven Business: How to Change the World, Make Money, and Have Fun* (Oakland, CA: Berrett-Koehler Publishers, 2008).
13 Meredith Davis, "Core Values Matter" *AIGA Design Futures Trend*, no. 4 (2018): 2.
14 Davis, "Core Values Matter," 1–2.
15 Tim Brown, *Change by Design* (New York: Harper, 2009), 3.
16 Sherry Hakimi, "Why Purpose-Driven Companies are Often More Successful." *Fast Company*, July 21, 2015.
17 "Carnegie Mellon School of Design framework," Carnegie Mellon University website, accessed January 4, 2019, http://design. cmu .edu /content /program -framework.
18 Willis, "Transition Design," 69–74.
19 Terry Irwin, "Transition Design: A Proposal for a New Era of Design Practice, Study and Research." Unpublished manuscript, School of Design, Carnegie Mellon University (2015): 2.
20 Caroline Gatt and Tim Ingold. "From Description to Correspondence: Anthropology in Real Time." In *Design Anthropology: Theory and Practice*, edited by Wendy Gunn, Ton Otto, and Rachel Smith (London: Bloomsbury, 2013), 139–158.
21 Terry Irwin, Gideon Kossoff, and Cameron Tonkinwise, "Transition Design Provocation," *Design Philosophy Papers* 13, no. 1 (2015): 3–11.
22 Escobar, 154.
23 Cameron Tonkinwise, "Design's (Dis)Orders and Transition Design," *Medium* (August 2014): 12, https://www.academia.edu/11791137/Design_Dis_Orders_Transition_Design_as_Postindustrial_Design.
24 Carroll, "Diversity & Inclusion in Design," 2.
25 AIGA, "Diversity & Inclusion: Learning Basics," accessed January 4, 2019, https://www.aiga.org/resources/diversity-inclusion-learning-basics.
26 Davis, "Complex Problems," 2.
27 Escobar, 40.
28 Paola Antonelli, keynote speech at the Solid Conference in 2014, "The New Frontiers of Design," published May 22, 2014, by O'Reilly Media, 14.10 min, https://www.YouTube.com/watch?v=u6mDAEOfGWQ.

29 Career Foundry, "What Is Typography, and Why Is It Important? [2023 Guide]," December 3, 2022, accessed January 11, 2022, https://careerfoundry.com/en/blog/ui-design/beginners-guide-to-typography/.

30 "Typography Design Guide: Why Is Typography Important?" Master Articles (last updated, June 16, 2021), accessed January 11, 2022, https://www.masterclass.com/articles/typography-design-guide.

31 "9 ridiculously good examples of kinetic typography | Inside Design Blog" (n.d.). 9 Ridiculously Good Examples of Kinetic Typography | Inside Design Blog, accessed January 11, 2022, https://www.invisionapp.com/inside-design/kinetic-typography-examples/.

32 Pelle Ehn, Elizabeth Nilsson, and Richard Topgaard, *Making Futures: Marginal Notes on Innovation, Design, and Democracy* (Cambridge, MA: MIT Press, 2014).

33 Boyuan Gaoand and Jahan Mantin, "How to Begin Designing for Diversity," Project Inkblot, accessed June 5, 2019, https://thecreativeindependent.com/guides/how-to-begin-designing-for-diversity.

34 Anthony Dunne and Fiona Raby, *Speculative Design: Design, Fiction, and Social Dreaming* (Cambridge, MA: MIT Press, 2013).

References

AIGA. "Diversity & Inclusion: Learning Basics." Accessed January 4, 2019. https://www.aiga.org/resources/diversity-inclusion-learning-basics.

Brown, Tim. Change by Design. New York: Harper, 2009.

Carrol, Antionette. "Diversity & Inclusion in Design: Why Do They Matter?" Accessed January 4, 2019. https://www.aiga.org/diversity-and-inclusion-in-design-why-do-they-matter.

Cohen, Ben and Mai Warwick. *Values-Driven Business: How to Change the World, Make Money, and Have Fun.* Oakland, CA: Berrett-Koehler Publishers, 2008.

Davis, Meredith. "Complex Problems," *AIGA Design Futures Trend,* no. 1 (2018a). Available at: https://www.aiga.org/sites/default/files/2021-02/Complex%20.

Davis, Meredith. "Aggregation and Curation," *AIGA Design Futures Trend,* no. 2 (2018b). Available at: https://www.aiga.org/sites/default/files/2023-09/Aggregation-and-Curation.pdf.

Davis, Meredith. "Core Values Matter," *AIGA Design Futures Trend,* no. 4 (2018c). Available at: https://www.aiga.org/sites/default/files/2021-02/Core%20Values%20Matter.pdf.

Dunne, Anthony and Fiona Raby. *Speculative Design: Design, Fiction, and Social Dreaming.* Cambridge, MA: MIT Press, 2013.

Ehn, Pelle, Elizabeth Nilsson and Richard Topgaard. *Making Futures: Marginal Notes on Innovation, Design, and Democracy.* Cambridge, MA: MIT Press, 2014.

Ehn, Pelle, Elizabeth Nilsson and Richard Topgaard. "Introduction." In *Making Futures: Marginal Notes on Innovation, Design, and Democracy,* edited by Pelle Ehn, Elizabeth Nilsson and Richard Topgaard, 1–16. Cambridge, MA: MIT Press, 2014.

Escobar, Arturo. *Designs for the Pluriverse: Radical Interdependence, Autonomy, and the Making of Worlds.* Durham, NC and London: Duke University Press, 2018.

Gaoand, Boyuan and Jahan Mantin. "How to Begin Designing for Diversity." Accessed June 5, 2019. https://thecreativeindependent.com/guides/how-to-begin-designing-for-diversity/.

Gaspar, Christine, and Liz Ogbu. 2015. "Using Our Words: The Language of Design for Equity." Next City. July 6, 2015. https://nextcity.org/urbanist-news/using-our-words-the-language-of-design-for-equity.

72 *Minjee Jeon*

Gatt, Caroline and Tim Ingold. "From Description to Correspondence: Anthropology in Real Time." In *Design Anthropology: Theory and Practice*, edited by Wendy Gunn, Ton Otto and Rachel Smith, 139–158. London: Bloomsbury, 2013.

Hakimi, Sherry. "Why Purpose-Driven Companies Are Often More Successful." *Fast Company*. July 21, 2015.

Irwin, Terry, Cameron Tonkinwise and Gideon Kossoff. "Transition Design Symposium Provocation." Carnegie Mellon School of Design, 2015. https://www. academia .edu /11439480 /Transition Design Symposium Provocation abbreviated version.

Irwin, Terry, Gideon Kossoff, Cameron Tonkinwise and Peter Scupelli. "Transition Design Bibliography." Unpublished manuscript, 2015. https://www.academia. edu/13108611/TransitionDesignBibliography, 2015.

Irwin, Terry, Gideon Kossoff and Cameron Tonkinwise. "Transition Design: An Educational Framework for Advancing the Study and Design of Sustainable Transitions." For the 6th International Sustainability Transitions Conference, University of Sussex, UK, August 2015.

Irwin, Terry, Gideon Kossoff and Cameron Tonkinwise. "Transition Design Provocation." *Design Philosophy Papers* 13 (2015): 3–11.

Irwin, Terry. "Transition Design: A Proposal for a New Era of Design Practice, Study and Research." Unpublished manuscript, School of Design, Carnegie Mellon University, 2015.

Kommonen, Kari-Hans. "Design Ecosystems and the Design of Everyday Life." Unpublished paper, Arki Group, Media Lab, Aalto University, Helsinki, 2013, http://www.scoop.it/t/design-of everyday-life.

Kommonen, Kari-Hans. "In Search of Digital Design." Unpublished manuscript, n.d. Media Lab, Aalto University, Helsinki.

Laurel, Brenda. *Design Research: Methods and Perspectives*. Cambridge, MA: MIT Press, ed. 2003.

Laurel, Brenda. "Introduction: Muscular Design." In *Design Research: Methods and Perspectives*, edited by Brenda Laurel, 16–19. Cambridge, MA: MIT Press, 2003.

Miller, Meg. 2017. "Survey: Design Is 73% White." Fast Company. January 31, 2017. https://www.fastcompany.com/3067659/survey-design-is-73-white. Accessed January 4, 2019.

Otto, Ton and Rachel Smith. "Design Anthropology: A Distinct Style of Knowing." In *Design Anthropology: Theory and Practice*, edited by Wendy Gunn, Ton Otto, and Rachel Smith, 1–31. London: Bloomsbury, 2013.

Scupelli, Peter. "Designed Transitions and What Kind of Design Is Transition Design?" *Design Philosophy Papers* 13 (2015): 75–84.

Thackara, John. *In the Bubble: Designing in a Complex World*. Cambridge, MA: MIT Press, 2004.

Tonkinwise, Cameron. "Design's (Dis)Orders and Transition Design." Medium. August 2014, https://www.academia.edu/11791137/Design_Dis_Orders_Transition_ Design_as_Postindustrial_Design.

Tonkinwise, Cameron. "Design for Transitions—from and to What?" *Design Philosophy Papers* 13, no. 1 (2015): 85–92.

Willis, Anne-Marie. "Transition Design: The Need to Refuse Discipline and Transcend Instrumentalism." *Design Philosophy Papers* 13, no. 1 (2015): 69–74.

5 Yame City

Cinema and Intangible Cultural Heritage through the Experience of Modernity

Sarah Mills

Introduction

Since its establishment in 1950, the concept of Intangible Cultural Heritage (ICH) has been widely recognised in Japanese society. The government supports practitioners of traditional craft techniques, folk customs and performing arts, with highly skilled individuals regarded as 'Ningen-Kokuho' (Living National Treasures). These individuals have encountered drastic social and cultural changes over the previous century but continue to engage in traditional practices in particular locations. This chapter questions how culture becomes recognised as ICH in Japan, and in what context people have, and continue to collectively practice, 'tradition' through their experience of modernity?

Cinematic Commons (MArch studio), travelled to Japan on the invitation of Kyushu University to mount our exhibition, 'A New Infrastructure of Subtraction for Tokyo' and to co-direct a workshop with Kyushu design students in Yame, Fukuoka Prefecture supported by Yame Chamber of Commerce and Industry. In Yame, Japanese traditional crafts such as Kurume Kasur (cotton cloth), Yame Chochin (paper lanterns), Yame Fukushima Butsudan (Buddhist alter), and Koishiwara yaki (pottery) are still manufactured and students stayed and worked in local machiya, while they researched and recorded these collective practices. The workshop and subsequent research hoped to uncover new technologies and collaborations using film analysis and film making to access, capture, analyse and propose possible spatial 'infrastructures' of collective value contributing to the transmission, safeguarding and development of ICH. The gaze and the take lay bare cultural form as tradition with the focus placed on several entities: practitioner, the work, production techniques, the consumer, and the space where the form originates, including the people who inhabit the space and their relationship to others.

As film directors such as Ozu, Yamanaka, and Sperry demonstrated, the conscious and reflective gaze of the camera lens opens up a new comprehension and imagination of urban and rural situations and patterns of spatial engagement but can ICH[1] be effectively safeguarded using forms of participatory or other forms of film making? Gibson-Graham's argument contained in

DOI: 10.4324/9781032616650-5

their project of reimagining "the power differential embedded in the binaries of global and local, space and place" is a reformulation of local identities.[2] Within our research we used essay film to question these ideas to focus on the reimagining of spaces and the social dimensions in which people identify themselves. ICH is a time-space practice that contains segmented memories of local people in their space, intersected with moments of exchange and it only appears as a result of a practitioner's action. The chapter discusses the impact of community building in Yame and the work undertaken by Machiya Revitalization Support Team, NPO Yame Townscape Design Study Group and Machizukuri Net Yame as well as the participatory film 'The Who's Who of the Machiya' produced by Hiroyuki Kawaida in Yame and the observational films of 'Unagino Nedoko'. The conclusion proposes a metamorphic character in the building and craft traditions in Yame, to reconsider possible relationships between existing residents and new visitors (whether on site or online), to demonstrate a social institution of 'tradition' in which the people can recognise the value of cultural form together by producing and consuming it (Figures 5.1 and 5.2).

Yame City and Community Building

Yame is located South of Fukuoka Prefecture, Japan. In the Fukushima area, traditional Japanese houses built in the Edo Period remain. Parts of Yame were damaged in the 1991 Typhoon Roke, following which Guidelines for Traditional Streetscape Maintenance and Improvement were developed for the Fukushima area to help residents repair and improve their environment based on their common agreements. In 1994, the Finance Bureau of Yame formed a Committee for Landscape Maintenance and Improvement for the Historic Neighbourhoods and made an Agreement on Community Building with the local residents.

In 1995 an Executive Committee of Historic Neighbourhood Conservation (ECHNC) was established whose board members included the heads of community associations and local residents in Fukushima.[3] ECHNC was part of the administrative system of the city; the Finance Bureau of Yame financed improvements and guided its community to protect and improve their Fukushima. According to the Agreement on Community Building, the owners of buildings and structures in a traditional Japanese style could receive a construction subsidy. With the support from Finance Bureau of Yame and local architects, the Guidelines on the Restoration and Improvement of Traditional Building and Streetscape in Historic Neighbourhood was published in 1998, which specified detailed objectives for the community building in Fukushima.[4] ECHNC also established a Steering Committee for architectural restoration and a Neighbourhood Design Research Committee with local architects in 2000. At the end of 2010, the Yame Cultural Landscape Plan was published,

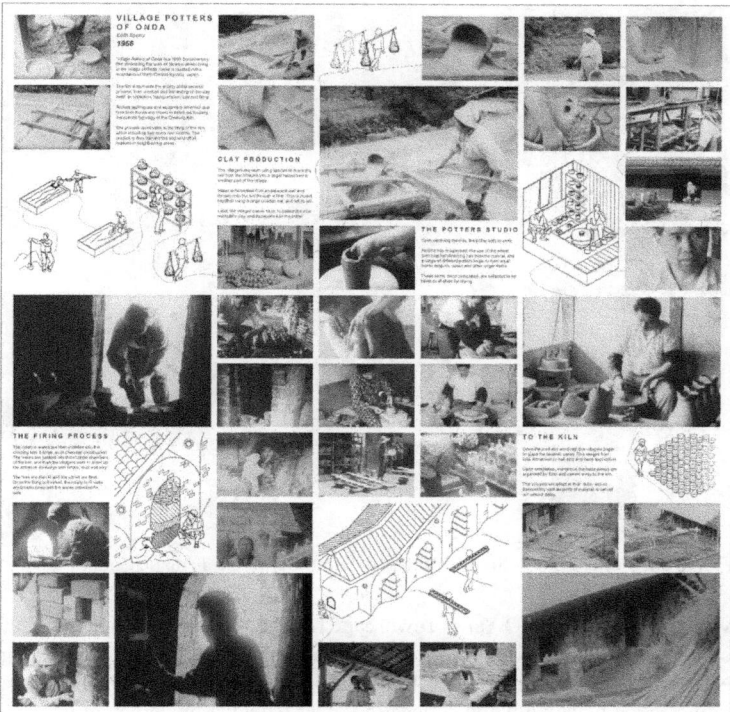

Figure 5.1 'Village Potters of Onda' Spatial Research, Matt Shepheard, Cinematic Commons.

in which a public-private partnership was introduced for the promotion of cultural landscape conservation.[5] A future vision of community building with landscape conservation and social sustainability was also proposed, facilitating an overall revitalisation of the local community via landscape maintenance and improvement in order to respond to the current situation of ageing population with fewer children in Japan.[6]

The National Federation of UNESCO Associations of Japan (NFUAJ) has been conducting a Future Heritage Campaign since 2009. The NFUAJ provides support to community activities to save local and cultural heritage and inscribes the outstanding community activities to the "Heritage for the Future Project List". In 2022, 73 projects are included from 37 prefectures nationwide, including 'Yame Fukushima: Inheritance of townscape culture by vacant townhouses and regeneration of traditional construction methods' led by Yame Machiya Revitalization Support Team who promote the reuse of

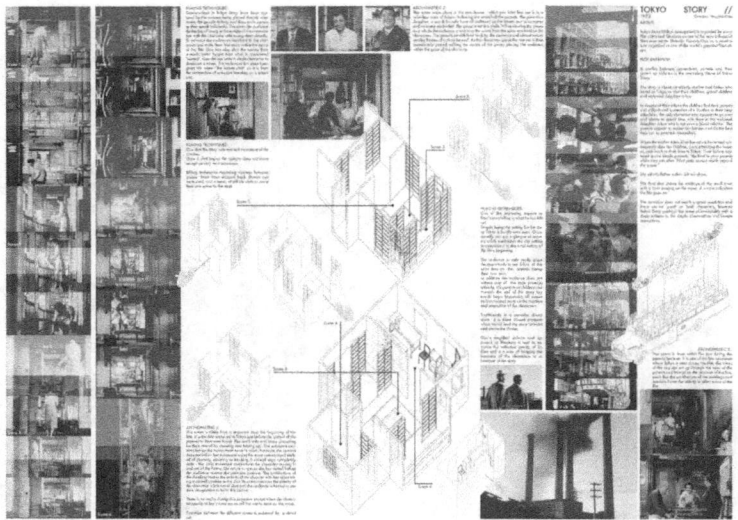

Figure 5.2 'Tokyo Story' Spatial Research, Sarah Gerrish, Cinematic Commons.

vacant houses and NPO Yame Townscape Design Study Group who facilitate education and transmission of traditional building techniques.[7] Machizukuri Net Yame brings together several local NPOs, and actively promotes restoration of local machiya while connecting older machiya owners with potential younger tenants, developing education and construction training and local business openings. In this project, Yame City also supports the activities of NPO corporations through government crowdfunding. Using the 'Donation Grant Guidelines for Supporting NPO Corporation Activities' which includes the Furusato Tax Payment allows communities to donate to their hometown or the local government.[8]

'The Who's Who of the Machiya'

Producer Hiroyuki Kawaida initiated the film 'The Who's Who of the Machiya' in 2012, fearing the slow activities of various parts of Japan are about to be abandoned. Kawaida comments that *"Here in Yame Fukushima, we have preserved the townscape and traditions by fostering a 'loose community"*.[9] Recording some of the activities related to 'Machizukuri Net Yame' and their impact on the Yame community were intended as a catalyst for his own activities based in Kyushu and would also highlight the possibilities in Yame for young people and those who have migrated from other areas trying to set a new direction. Working with Yame Machiya Revitalization Support

Team and NPO Yame Townscape Design Study Group the film documents a year in Yame, Fukushima, a location which shares its name with the site of an ongoing nuclear tragedy in northeast Japan. Yuki Ito, the director, filmed the slow process of restoring various carefully crafted old structures and realised that the time required in their restoration enables those who are involved in the work to confirm the values they share and to further build upon their connections with one another. In Yame, Yuki Ito questions what we gain from progress, what we lose and if the machiya should be preserved, rebuilt, or simply be disregarded? There were difficulties in the production process due to the necessity of approvals from locals, many of whom feature in the film, asking if making a movie would help protect the landscape of the city but it was necessary to make the film local and "*After many discussions a production committee was formed and the local screening was successful*".[10] The film readdresses the options of post-war Japan from the perspective of the region and records people's struggles to revitalise machiya which are at the mercy of modernisation and efficiency, by capturing "*the subtleties of life inherent in machiya and the people who live there*" throughout the year.[11]

Kyu Yame Gun-Yakusho (Former Yame District Office) features in 'The Who's Who of the Machiya' prior to its later Machizukuri Net Yame led repair. In the film, the future of this large-scale building is discussed. The first idea was to gradually repair the building with the prepaid rent paid by the first store to open following partial restoration with other funds to be received via membership fees to the corporation, donations from people who supported the activities, 'Housing and Community Foundation Housing and Community Building Activities' subsidy, 'Taisei Construction Natural Environment and History Fund' and 'Yame City Unoccupied House Regeneration/Utilization Model Project'.[12] Built between 1900 and 1918, the original District Office is an unusually large wooden structure which has also been used as a refined wax factory, military munitions factory and hattori feed store but after years of no use the owners of the building and associated land offered the building to Yame City in June 2006. However, even if the city accepted the donation, it was difficult to find the funds for its restoration and a prospect for its utilisation.[13] A partial restoration took until 2017 to complete and the building now houses a bookshop, drinks store and community events space while outside there are community-maintained gardens. Much of the restoration has been carried out by the local community and visiting groups not necessarily the master craftspeople who undertook the repair of the local machiya and this led to a different outcome but also many opportunities for the community to be involved (Figure 5.3).

Recent installations within Gun-Yakusho's largest space, the 25 × 10 metre large hall, include Paramodel's, Yasuhiko Hayashi Joint Factory installation of 2018 and Takarajima Dyeing Industries Project, Makuma (Kukai) of 2019; both projects embrace the scale and height of the timber structure. Paramodel's title comes from the combination of the words,

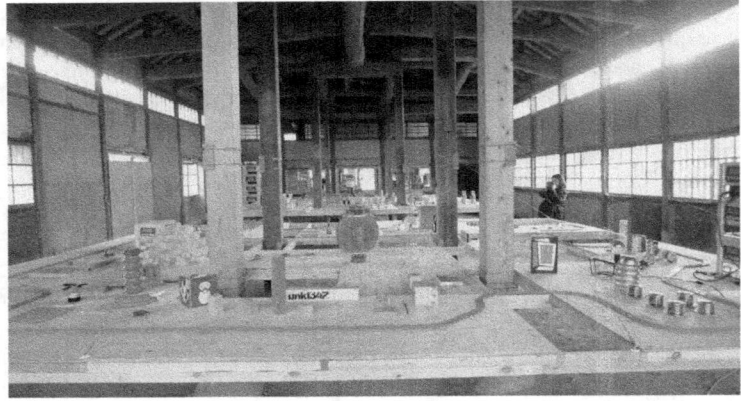

Figure 5.3 Joint Factory Installation, Paramodel, "Kyu Yame Gun-Yakusho", Yame, Japan, 2018.

'paradise' and 'model', and the fusion of these two concepts is essentially the launching point of their creations. They manage to work in parallel towards the same vision of constructing intricate models of 'paradise' using everyday objects, toy parts, like plastic train tracks and mini-cars. Engaging in this poetic, yet paradoxical practice of remodelling paradise in this case elevated on a platform, away from the building's dirt floor. A model train negotiates the terrain and various everyday objects which following the building's partial restoration talks directly to the opportunities unfolding as a result of its community's action.

In Takarajima Dyeing Industries Project, visitors experience various dyeing techniques via carefully hung materials and clothes exhibited to frame particular activities within the hall while also celebrating the atmospheres of the building. Silhouettes created behind cotton layers suggest building histories as well as possible new spaces. Harking back to the building's previous uses, the manual and traditional process of wax resist dyeing is transformed (Figure 5.4).

Yame Fukushima no Toro Ningyo, the lantern dolls of Yame Fukushima, is a string-and-pole manipulated mechanical puppet tradition in Fukushima Hachiman Shrine. The festival has continued since its conception in 1744 and has been designated an 'Intangible Folk and Cultural Asset' by the Japanese government. The 'actors' performing on stage are all karakuri mechanical dolls who perform pieces of classical Japanese theatre; each one is operated by a crew of 18 people situated below and to the side of the stage. The dolls themselves are string-less, and are instead controlled by a series of rods and pulleys under the stage that are fixed to the base of the doll. Altogether, a single performance takes a crew of 100 volunteers. In the 'The Who's Who of the

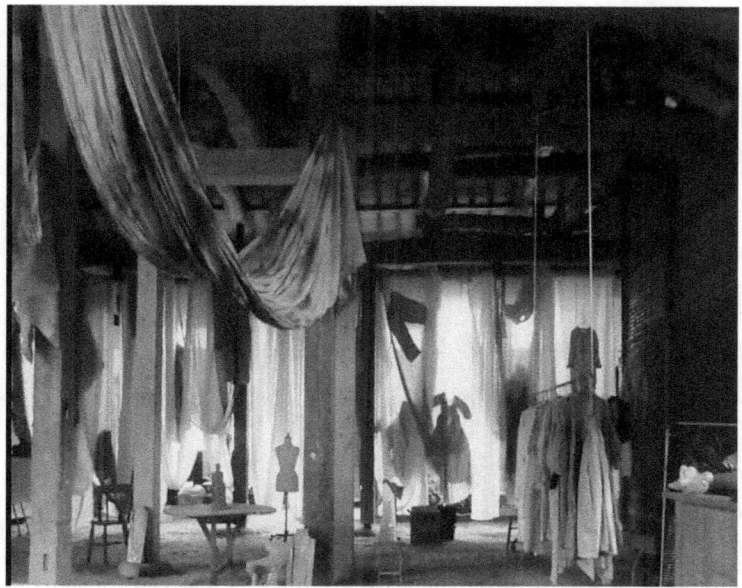

Figure 5.4 Takarajima Dyeing Industries Project, "Kyu Yame Gun-Yakusho", Yame, Japan, 2019.

Machiya' film, Yame residents carefully construct the temporary stage for this unique puppet performance within the area of their local shine demonstrating another established time-based and shared practice which helps heighten the sense of community.[14] The timber construction is fourteen metres high and assembled without the use of any screws or nails. Due to the yearly tradition, the stage is dismantled after just one week. In the film, the viewers gaze is manoeuvred away from the stage directly towards the audience to the hands of the puppets' operators.

'The Who's Who of the Machiya' is a form of participatory cinema where the dynamics of the filmmaking process are acknowledged, and the subjects of the film were allowed to project their culture directly on film. Here, the filmmaker is part of the ethnographic situation and part of the film event. Anthropological knowledge is being created through dialogue, exchange and interrelation between individuals and members of diverse cultures.[15] Participatory cinema and collaborative films involve conversation and the creation of conditions that allow for the generation of knowledge, rather than the exchange of existing information. Participatory cinema generates platforms for the articulation of the subject's points of view, as well as the support of their needs and aspirations (Figure 5.5).

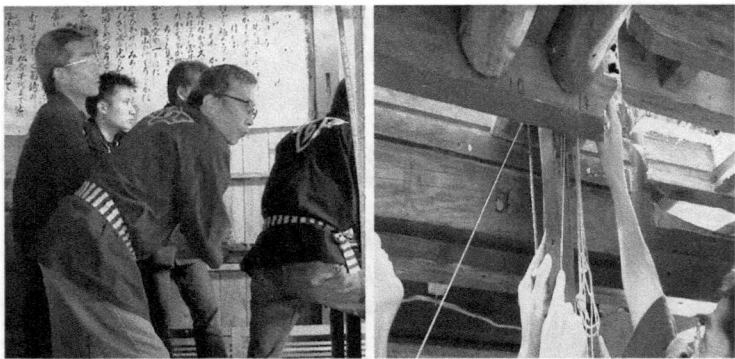

Figure 5.5 Film Stills: Yame Fukushima no Toro Ningyo in 'The Who's Who of the Machiya', 2013.

Unagino Nedoko

The 'Eel Bed Building', Yame is a former lantern shop called Marubayashi Honke which was restored and rented by Unagino Nedoko, a company initiated by Takahiro Shiramizu. Shiramizu worked on 'The Who's Who of the Machiya' film and edited an associated publication, 'Machizukuri',[16] originally trained as an architect his trading company now uses film to promote the region. The films such as 'Kurume Kasuri - Japanese Ikat', 2016 expose Japanese traditional crafts from the Yame and beyond, including practitioners, works, production techniques, timescales, and importantly the space and landscape where the form originates and their relationship to others. Shiramizu has catalogued particular craft workshops and local producers via area or region and plotted these via maps to form critical 'constellations'[17] rooted to materials and neighbouring landscapes in Kyushu. Unagino Nedoko's goals are to interpret an edited range of local culture and explore ways to utilise it today; creating a continuous economic cycle and practice a mechanism to return profits to local culture. The company has four stores, a collaboration/ workshops space, publishing, and has recently opened an inn. Experiencing the renovated machiya in Yame forms part of the experience of purchasing products. Shiramizu plans to communicate with society by looking at the value of "*regionalisation including manufacturing, town development, internationalisation, etc.*"[18] via establishing mechanisms for permeation (producers), connecting, and utilising local resources and nature.

The film 'Kurume Kasuri - Japanese Ikat' opens with the scene in an indigo dyeing workshop and the camera tracks the floor across eight circular vats containing the sukumo, coal, sugar, and lye liquid. The silence is only disturbed by clock ticking, liquid indigo being stirred, or the slams of the yarn against concrete: repeated 50 times as part of the process. The camera stays fixed in

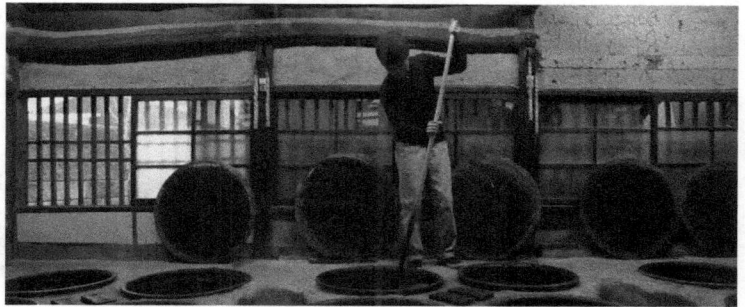

Figure 5.6 Film Still: 'Kurume Kasuri - Japanese Ikat', 2017.

position for the first half of the 30-minute film and the solitude of working in the atelier process is expressed. Scenes of the indigo dying process, making fire beds to maintain temperatures essential for fermentation, washing, sun drying and untying the yarn, warp beaming and weaving in the handloom reveal different workshop spaces but their relationship to the dyeing workshop isn't revealed. Part-documentary, part-educational, part-promotional, the process of making the cloth and the film is considered above any future narrative or possible connection to the community. The film was made in Mr. Takeshi Yamamura's Aizome Kasuri Atelier, who specialises in natural indigo-dyed, hand-woven kasuri. 'Kurume Kasuri' a traditional cotton textile which has a 200-year history, woven in Chikugo area of Southern Fukuoka and registered as ICH by UNESCO in 1957.[19] 'Kasuri' is a Japanese tie-dye technique equivalent to 'ikat', which creates patterns by partially binding the yarn before dyeing and weaving. It is considered to be a technique originated in India, and came to Japan in the early 15th century through Okinawa, and spread to mainland Japan, including Kurume. There are still about 30 Kurume kasuri weavers in the area, and they are all unique in style (Figure 5.6).

The Unagino Nedoko films can be compared with films such as 'Village Potters of Onda' directed by Edith Sperry in 1966. Sperry records the activities and ways of life of Japanese folk potters in Onda, a remote village in the mountains of North Central Kyushu. This film presents a detailed account of traditional pottery-making techniques which have remained relatively unchanged for more than 250 years, with 9 families in village making pottery with the uphill stoking of progressive kiln chambers being particular unique. However, Sperry's film is successful in exploring some of the ecological, social, political, and economic issues of this specific location.

Unlike the participatory filmic practices undertaken in 'The Who's Who of the Machiya' which reflect the community and practices of Machizukuri, the Unagino Nedoko film audience is expected to immerse itself in the event through the reception of the film. In an ethnographic context this methodology was termed observational cinema.[20] Here the invisible camera is located at a distance and forms a demarcation line. As discussed widely in papers at the 2014 conference 'Documenting Intangible Cultural Heritage on Film' in this context the filmmaker is conceptualised as omnipotent, able to grasp an event in its totality and to give evidence of it. Here the filmmaker neglecting their presence and the camera used in the pursuit of knowledge. On the Unagino Nedoko website a data base compiles their observational films to form collections which are linked to a mapping of their geographical locations as well as particular crafts. Overall, the content may suggest a 'commoning' community and ecological cohesion but also opens up other questions of copyrights.

Cinematic Commons

'The Who's Who of the Machiya' and 'Unagino Nedoko' films engaged the Yame community during planning, production, at community film screenings and online via open access. Group Gendai Films also enter their films to be screened as part of film festivals to engage global communities and expose issues related to the future of Yame's (in)tangible heritage plus the impact of the current ecological, political, and social contexts. However, what are the pedagogical values of film analysis, as part of the fieldwork methodology within an architecture design studio and can other filmic observations and associated methods of engagement and film production be valuable as a design tool?

The 'Cinematic Construct of New Commons' is a MArch studio at Leeds School of Architecture initiated in 2013/2014 by Sarah Mills and Doreen Bernath. The associated research project and network have traversed urban contexts from Mumbai, Mexico City, Tokyo, Marseilles, London, Berlin to Beijing, and questions the assumed opposition between the immateriality of films and the material basis of architecture. It critically unravels a possible shared domain of 'scenic' constructs which can be considered both as the material artifice of films and the immaterial confluence of architectural spaces. As a force of subversion, the intrusion of filmic observations and interventions on cities began to provoke and make visible what were deliberately omitted in earlier modes of urbanism.[21]

In 2017/2018, the 'Infrastructure of Ningen Kojuhu' titled design studio brief located the project in Japan for the second year running. A November fieldtrip included visits to buildings in Kyoto,[22] a presentation of our research Kyoto Design Lab – Kyoto Institute of Technology, Matsugasaki and a visit to the archipelago of the Setouchi Islands to investigate the international festival which foregrounds a new type of relationship between culture and 'corporations' to promote ideas such as regional revitalisation through art, the concept of public capitalism.[23] We mounted our exhibition 'A New Infrastructure of Subtraction for Tokyo' collaborating with KID NEXT (Kyudai Innovation

Design NEXT) at Kyushu University Faculty of Design before travelling to Yame City for the remainder of the trip.

Entry into urbanism via film through the 'foreign gaze' began prior to the Japan trip via analysis of a Japanese filmography linked to important Architectural events[24] and students worked together to produce analytical 'space boards', for each film to reflect analysis of the film scenes. The content included a mixture of stills, sequences, spatial analytical drawings in the form of simple axo/isos, plans/sections. The focus on creative production was (in)tangible heritage and its transmission, the scenes, characters, rituals, and stories being between two or more spaces. The challenge was to make visible the juxtapositions of these contexts. Students were encouraged to observe and record camera positions, viewing angles/range, depth and layers of space, manipulations in time, visible or invisible presences of sounds or bodies, movements of cameras and scenes, strategies of tracking, panning, sequencing and cuts. By collecting clips of chosen scenes and sequences, they began a version of an 'essay film', though the 'foreign gaze' which started to consider how experiential and durational information can be captured and represented in the filmic medium. Other aspects considered for the creation of an initial essay film included meditation on a theme (substituted for plot); disunity of time, space, tone, materials, style; modularity; suspension of belief; self-criticism/ self-reflexivity; non-anticipatory camera and varied editing strategies.

As Laura Rascaroli (2009) discusses in her book *The Personal Camera: Subjective Cinema and The Essay Film*, the subject who sees the world through the camera lens is a precarious but inquisitive subject. The subject is not necessarily a vulnerable one but a political subject who attempts to affect the viewer by generating proximity between the narratives on the screen and the viewer by his or her intimate tones of voice. The return to political and cultural events in the essay film is that which makes possible the construction of the 'foreign gaze' with the power to straddle fiction and non-fiction, and at the same time, to be concretely personal. The 'foreignness' includes the revisiting of the past and re-documentation in the present juxtaposing both the personal reinterpretation and the rejigging of collective memory and meaning. Shanay Jhaveri, the editor of Outsider Films on India 1950–1990, explains the two-fold role of the 'foreign gaze' as that which is '*no only a fascinating mediation of foreignness, but also an intriguing re-assessment of the cultural history of a society*'.

In Yame, Design students from Kyushu University with Minako Ikeda and Master of Architecture students from Leeds School of Architecture participated in a workshop together while staying in renovated Yame Machiya, including the previously mentioned 'Unagino Nedoko'. The Traditional Craft Centre built by Yame City in 1986 for the purpose of developing local industries was one of the workshop sites. The centre contains examples of nationally designated traditional crafts and specialty crafts/folk crafts. It was built on the site of the former JR Yabe Line Chikugo-Fukushima Station. The abolished

Japanese National Railways Yabe Line is remembered with a production that runs through the museum.[25] The Centre is linked to the Handmade Japanese Paper Museum and the Yame Folk Museum. Workshop participants attended talks by members of the Yame Machiya Revitalization Support Team and NPO Yame Townscape Design Study Group and discussed together the possibilities for the future of the Traditional Craft and the potential of the Centre to connect with the local communities.

In her paper 'Scaffold for designing modern products by reinterpreting the technique and philosophy of traditional crafts', Minako Ikeda, proposes it is essential to reinterpret traditional craft of Japan in the modern context, keeping the essence of tradition. Ikeda and Kyushu Social Communication Design students used Koishiwara Pottery and Yame-Fukushima Buddhist Altar manufacturing as a starting point for their research, conducted studies on their historical background, observations of manufacturing techniques and processes to build a framework or scaffold to help analyse the techniques and background of traditional crafts and reinterpret them to design products in the modern context. Based on reinterpretations, a series of prototypes of modern tableware were developed based on traditional techniques and thoughts in the context of modern life. Using wood cutting and processing, lacquering, and gold gilding techniques used in making the Buddhist altars and efficient delicate forms for plates, manufacturing variations and various lacquering techniques are proposed to bring a new value in modern life.[26]

The proposed 'scaffold' in the Yame workshop became spatial and incorporated filmic techniques to access, capture, analyse and propose possible spatial 'infrastructures' of collective value contributing to the transmission, safeguarding and development of ICH. Further, the potential for spaces to be translated and reinterpreted for different contexts over time, or infrastructures scaled up or reconnected and the impact on the current and future communities were discussed addressed.

Direct film methods were used initially to collect footage of the makers, materials, production techniques and the particular spaces associated with the production of handmade washi paper and Chochin lanterns in Yame. Gathering material using methods of direct cinema reduces required equipment to bare essentials, using handheld cameras and attempting to make oneself unobtrusive; however, allowing life to unfold before the camera in reality was challenging. Turning next to observational cinema, the camera was not confined to a passive role but was used for personal exploration where the workshop film makers became an active user creating a self-conscious form of cinema (Figure 5.7).

Students from Leeds and Kyushu also worked in groups becoming screen writers to make comparisons with the creative process of the architect, to build new ways of seeing and expressing ideas from tools used in cinema. Storyboards proposed strategic infrastructures to spatially connect the makers of traditional crafts in Yame and create opportunities for exchange. Associated

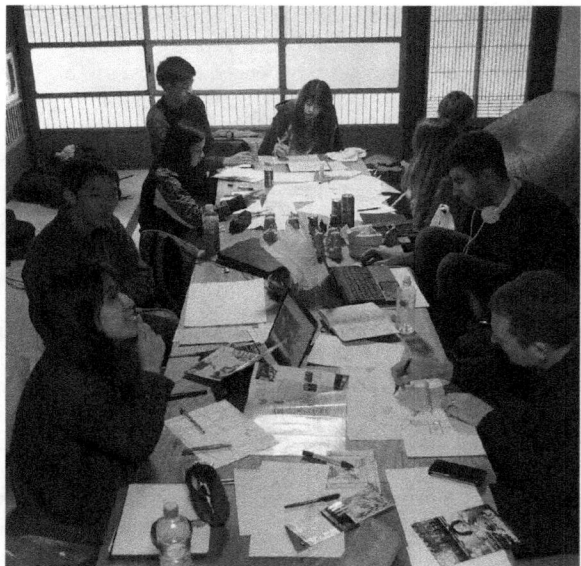

Figure 5.7 Leeds School of Architecture and Kyushu University students in Yame.

timelines encompassed flashbacks, flash forwards, shifting perspectives, alternate outcomes, multiple timelines, and time travel. Planned films asked the questions: What is the shared identity and necessary actions to instigate a position of mutual 'commonness' to those gathered in a space/time situation or a shared purpose? How can continuity be established through recognisable reoccurrences on the chosen site? How can collective actions support the reinterpretation of traditional craft of Japan in the modern context, keeping the essence of tradition? Workshop participants interrogated the domain of imageries traversing architectural, urban planning, and film-making practices related to (in)tangible heritage, and researched the intensive and extensive film industry revealed through filmic documentation and architectural analyses in the organisation of spaces, activities, people, resources, production, and distribution.

In Yame a hidden 'commoning' culture associated with its tangible and intangible heritage was revealed via an exploration of films produced in and around Yame which identified reformers looking beyond the state (and the city) to sub-local forms of cooperation or resistance to make claim on resources, asserting the existence of a common stake or common interest in resources shared with other inhabitants as a way of resisting commodification of those resources ultimately challenging issues of scale and issues of enclosure but at an operational level, also retaining a 'local autonomy' that is non-hierarchical and non-commodified and shared.

For students the physical experience of living and working within Yame Machiya was invaluable. New time-based rituals such negotiating various thresholds and screen devices as experienced via Ozu's 'Tokyo Story' pre trip or working in groups on low timber chabudai, unfolding and refolding tatami mats, all while understanding the impact of environmental changes and societal values on these buildings. Ultimately over the six months following the Japan trip 'Cinematic Commons' developed design projects between Kyoto and Yame mediated through a combination of filmic, essayistic, and scenographic constructs – of what is real and what is 'common' – as a new approach to architecture-making. By turning to cultural and political events in the immediate or distant pasts and repeatedly offering new takes, the film essay was developed to comment and criticise representational assumptions via design projects deviating from the dichotomy of fiction and documentary by commanding a voice that can form or un-form images. Modes of observational cinema initially had a distinctive role to play in expanding research imagination, reaching new audiences, and producing unique material or cultural artefacts however interpretations of 'the real' inner landscapes of the imagination not just external events need to be considered when using film methods. This is why the mode of essay film was ultimately developed within the studio to communicate projects; this distinction is made by the Deleuzian conception of the 'time-image' as a variant that is located in the space of thought and imagination.[27] Significant is the change in the nature and scope of the 'architectural project', as pondered through films, acts, and scenes from the intricacies of the process, assisting tools, decision-making criteria, expected outcomes to modes of engagement and associated implications.

Conclusion

This chapter proposes a metamorphic character in the building and craft traditions in Yame City, using film as a way to reconsider possible relationships between past and present and new visitors (whether residents, cultural 'tourists', local new businesses or digitally online). Participatory cinema and collaborative films involve conversation and the creation of conditions that allow for the generation of knowledge, rather than the exchange of existing information. ICH manifests itself through the recognition of the local communities, groups and individuals and this cultural contextualisation and significance also needs to be addressed within representation via film if it aims to acknowledge and (re)narrate. Community participation can be efficiently used to strengthen common identity and to creatively influence the representation of ICH. The films discussed expose how Machizukuri, in Yame's context, focuses on a model of community management characterised by agreements between diverse organisations joining efforts with community cooperation platforms to resolve problems in a more comprehensive way. Assumptions that ICH is a social norm through which people respect 'tradition' and expect it to be safeguarded for its own sake as a counter value of modernity, and globalisation have been challenged. The community activities in Yame reconsider ICH as a cultural form of living human activity in an ever-changing society, shared by people as a result of modernity. ICH is traditional and contemporary; it adapts and changes in line with changing socio-cultural environments, is constantly in a state of becoming and it forms a constituent part of the cultural identity of the respective communities, groups, and individuals. 'The Who's Who of the Machiya' film discussed people's struggles with technological choices, and the number of trails and errors undergone in the process of reviving Yame for the next generation. Unagino Nedoko films highlight the metamorphic character of 'traditional craft products' empowered by the market economy to create exchange value in the realm of 'tradition'. Both demonstrate an oscillation of relations between past and present, as part of the production processes but Yame has selected a most appropriate means by which to employ 'tradition' and to mediate the values of 'self' and 'other'. 'Cinematic Commons' architecture design studio discovered in Yame, via filmic investigations and modes of production, a hidden-commons; the potential of film as a tool to unearth new knowledge and to communicate a shared understanding of spaces and importantly to change the scope of the 'architectural project' via acts and scenes to imaginatively propose collective futures with implications on both ordinary and extraordinary dimensions of everyday life.

Notes

1 See Ozu Yasujirō's 'Tokyo Story', 1957, Sadao Yamanaka's 'Humanity and Paper Balloons', 1937 and Edith Sperry's 'Village Potters of Onda', 1966.
2 Katherine Gibson and Julie Graham, "Beyond Global vs. Local: Economic Politics Outside the Binary Frame," in *Geographies of Power: Placing Scale*, ed. Andrew Herod and Melissa W. Wright (Oxford: Blackwell, 2002), 29.
3 Noriaki Nishiyama, Yoko Omori and Ai Koguchi, "Conservation of Historical Townscape and Landscape by the Ordinance to Control Cultural Landscape: Case of Yame-City, Fukuoka Prefecture," *Journal of the City Planning Institute of Japan* 38, no. 3 (2003): 566.
4 Executive Committee of Historic Neighbourhood Conservation in Fukushima, Repair Manual of the Streetscape in Yame Fukushima District. Fukushima: Executive Committee of Historic Neighbourhood Conservation in Fukushima (2008).
5 Riki Kitajima, "Development of Landscape Planning Utilizing Cultural Heritage: From the Site of Yame Fukushima," accessed July 23, 2022, http://www.yame-machiya.info/wp-content/uploads/2016/08/2139ef8a21939901549cf319d49b46a6.pdf.
6 Xiang Zhou, "Development and Practices of Community Neighbourhood Conservation-Based Community Building in Japan," *Landscape Architecture Frontiers* 5, no. 5 (October 2017): 10, Gale Academic OneFile, accessed July 28, 2022, https://link.gale.com/apps/doc/A567634243/AONE?u=lmu_web&sid=google Scholar&xid=f2eee125.
7 National Federations of Unesco Federations in Japan, "World Heritage Activities and Heritage for the Future Project," accessed July 23, 2022. https://www.unesco.or.jp/activities/isan/heritage-for-the-future-project/.

8 Government Crowdfunding, "Yame Fukushima Machiya Preservation and Utilization Project [3rd] -Support for Machiya Revitalization in Nishikonyamachi," accessed July 23, 2022, https://www.furusato-tax.jp/gcf/1521.

9 Town Development net Yame, "The Who's Who of Machiya," accessed July 23, 2022, http://www.yame-machiya.info/%e5%88%b6%e4%bd%9c%e8%80%85%e3%81%ae%e3%81%93%e3%81%a8%e3%81%b0/.

10 Town Development net Yame, "The Who's Who of Machiya," accessed July 23, 2022.

11 Town Development net Yame, "The Who's Who of Machiya," accessed July 23, 2022.

12 Kurume Institute of Technology, "Former Yame Government Office Survey Report," 2011, Yame Cultural Promotion Organisation, accessed July 20, 2022, http://yame-machiya.net/wp-content/uploads/2011/11/gunyakusho.pdf.

13 Ayaka Uchino and Koji Kato, "Kyu Yame Gun-Yakusho," *Establishment, Reports to the City Planning Institute of Japan*, no. 17 (2018): 91.

14 Barbara E. Thornbury, "Puppets on Strings and Actors on Floats: Japan's Traditional Performing Arts in a Festival Setting," *The Journal of the Association of Teachers of Japanese* 26, no. 2 (1992): 189.

15 Anna Grimshaw, "Visual Anthropology," in *A New History of Anthropology*, ed. Henrika Kuklick (Malden: Blackwell, 2008), 293.

16 Takahiro Shiramizu, *Fukuoka Yame Fukushima Town Development Record* (Yame: Eel Bed Books, 2015), 5–8.

17 Constellating, as a mode of both material and conceptual rearrangements, transposed into formal methodologies of collage, montage and assemblage, permeated Benjamin's writings on photography, film and speculative scenes of experiences in cities. Howard Eiland and Michael W. Jennings (ed.), *Walter Benjamin's Selected Writings, Vol. 1* (Cambridge, MA and London: Harvard University Press, 1991–1999) and Graeme Gilloch, *Walter Benjamin, Critical Constellations* (Cambridge and New York: Polity Press, 2002).

18 Takahiro Shiramizu, "Introduction to Unagino Nedoko," accessed July 20, 2022, https://unagino-nedoko.net/about/.

19 The Inventory of Intangible Cultural Heritage in Japan, 2009, accessed July 20, 2022, https://ich.unesco.org/doc/src/02780-EN.pdf.

20 Colin Young, "Observational Cinema," in *Principles of Visual Anthropology*, ed. Paul Hockings (New York and Berlin: Mouton de Gruyter, 2003), 99.

21 Doreen Bernath and Sarah Mills, "Infrastitial Scenes - Constellating and Grafting" Architecture & Film Symposium proceedings, Ball State University and Washington State University (2021): 71.

22 Building visits included: Kanjiro Kawai's home and studio.

23 Soichiro Fukutake, "My Vision of the Seto Inland Sea," in *Insular Insight*, ed. Lars Muller and Akiko Miki (Zurich: Lars Mullers, 2012), 29.

24 Filmography included the following Japanese films aligned to architectural events such as Westernisation of Japanese Architecture; Post war reconstruction; futuristic theories on the city; social structure and changes in Japan as global cities emerge – Y. Ozu (1929), *I Graduated, But...*, Japan; Y. Ozu (1932), *I Was Born, But...*, Japan; I. Takahata (1988), *Grave of the Fireflies*, Japan; S. Yamanaka (1937), *Humanity and Paper Balloons*, Japan; A. Kurosawa (1960), *The Bad Sleep Well*, Japan; Y. Ozu (1953), *Tokyo Story*, Japan; J. Sargent (1977), *MacHartur*, USA; Suzuki Seijun (1966), *Tokyo Drifter*, Japan; T. Yamazaki (2005), *Always Sunset on Third Street*; K. Hasegawa (1976), *Youth to Kill*, Japan; K. Hasegawa (1979), *The Man Who Stole The Sun*, Japan; M. Noda (2003), *Tokyo Vein*, Japan; K. Omori (1991), *Gojira Tai Kingu Gidora*, Japan; N. Yoshinaga (2002), *Parasite Dolls*, Japan; W. Wenders (1985), *TokyoGa*, USA, West Germany; R. Hagenberg and NeubertKarl

(2001), *SurFACE*, Japan; J. Ichikawa (1995), *The Tokyo Siblings*, Japan; K. Mitani (2001), *Minna No Ie*, Japan; T. Okawara (1999), *Gojirani-sen Mireniamu*, Japan; K. Ootomo (1988), *Akira*, Japan; K. Satoshi (2003), *Tokyo Godfathers*, Japan; I. Takahata (1994), *Pom Poko*, Japan; S. Tsukamoto (1988), *Tetsuo I (Iron Man)*, Japan.

25 Yame Traditional Crafts Center, accessed 5 January 2023, https://yamedentouk-ougeikan.jimdo.com/.

26 Minako Ikeda, "Scaffold for Designing Modern Products by Reinterpreting the Technique and Philosophy of Traditional Crafts," IASDR 2017.

27 Giles Deleuze, *Cinema 2: The Time-Image*, trans. Hugh Tomlinson and Robert Galeta (London: Continuum, 2005).

References

Bernath, Doreen and Sarah Mills. "Infrastitial Scenes – Constellating and Grafting." Architecture & Film Symposium proceedings. Ball State University and Washington State University, 2021.

Deleuze, Giles. *Cinema 2: The Time-Image*. Translated by Hugh Tomlinson and Robert Galeta. London: Continuum 2005.

Eiland, Howard and Michael W. Jennings (Eds.). *Walter Benjamin's Selected Writings, Vol. 1*. Cambridge, MA and London: Harvard University Press, 1991–1999.

Executive Committee of Historic Neighbourhood Conservation in Fukushima. Repair Manual of the Streetscape in Yame Fukushima District. Fukushima: Executive Committee of Historic Neighbourhood Conservation in Fukushima, 2008.

Fukutake, Soichiro. "My Vision of the Seto Inland Sea." In *Insular Insight*, edited by Lars Muller and Akiko Miki, 29. Zurich: Lars Mullers, 2012.

Gibson, Katherine and Julie Graham. "Beyond Global vs. Local: Economic Politics Outside the Binary Frame." In *Geographies of Power: Placing Scale*, edited by Andrew Herod and Melissa W. Wright, 25–60. Oxford: Blackwell, 2002.

Gilloch, Graeme. *Walter Benjamin, Critical Constellations*. Cambridge and New York: Polity Press, 2002.

Grimshaw, Anna. "Visual Anthropology." In *A New History of Anthropology*, edited by Henrika Kuklick, 293–310. Malden: Blackwell, 2008.

Ikeda, Minako "Scaffold for Designing Modern Products by Reinterpreting the Technique and Philosophy of Traditional Crafts." International Association of Societies of Design Research Conference, 2017.

Kitajima, Riki. "Development of Landscape Planning Utilizing Cultural Heritage: From the Site of Yame Fukushima." Accessed July 23, 2022. http://www.yame-machiya.info/wp-content/uploads/2016/08/2139ef8a21939901549cf319d49b46a6.pdf.

Kurume Institute of Technology. "Former Yame Government Office Survey Report," 2011, Yame Cultural Promotion Organisation. Accessed July 20, 2022. http://yame-machiya.net/wp-content/uploads/2011/11/gunyakusho.pdf.

National Federations of UNESCO in Japan. "World Heritage Activities and Heritage for the Future Project." Accessed July 23, 2022. https://www.unesco.or.jp/activities/isan/heritage-for-the-future-project/.

Nishiyama, Noriaki, Yoko Omori and Ai Koguchi. "Conservation of Historical Townscape and Landscape by the Ordinance to Control Cultural Landscape: Case of Yame-City. Fukuoka Prefecture." *Journal of the City Planning Institute of Japan* 38, no. 3 (2003): 565–570.

90   *Sarah Mills*

Shiramizu, Takahiro. *Fukuoka Yame Fukushima Town Development Record.* Yame: Eel Bed Books, 2015.

Sperry, Edith. Director. *Village Potters of Onda.* Japan: The Japan Society, 1966.

Thornbury, Barbara E. "Puppets on Strings and Actors on Floats: Japan's Traditional Performing Arts in a Festival Setting." *The Journal of the Association of Teachers of Japanese* 26, no. 2 (1992): 189.

Town Development net Yame. "The Who's Who of Machiya." Accessed July 23, 2022. http://www.yame-machiya.info/.

Uchino, Ayaka and Koji Kato. "Kyu Yame Gun-Yakusho Establishment." *Reports to the City Planning Institute of Japan,* 17 (2018): 91.

UNESCO. "Convention Concerning the Protection of the World Cultural and Natural Heritage." Paris, 1972. Accessed July 23, 2022. http://whc.unesco.org/en/conventiontext/.

Young, Colin. "Observational Cinema." In *Principles of Visual Anthropology,* edited by Paul Hockings, 115–132. New York and Berlin: Mouton de Gruyter, 2003.

Zhou, Xiang. "Development and Practices of Community Neighbourhood Conservation-Based Community Building in Japan." *Landscape Architecture Frontiers* 5, no. 5 (October 2017): 10. Gale Academic OneFile. Accessed July 28, 2022. https://link.gale.com/apps/doc/A567634243/AONE?u=lmu_web&sid=googleScholar&xid=f2eee125.

6 The Relationship of Community and Commerce in Forming the Identity of Place

Lisa Phillips

Introduction

In ancient times, the Greek Agora and the Roman Forum were areas of assembly in which commerce was an essential element. In these spaces, people shopped while they participated "...in discussions concerning wider society"[1] and learned of news affecting public life. In cities like ancient Rome, other stores throughout the urban sprawl were also available to address the needs of the diverse population. For the commoners, simple shops, tabernae, sold a variety of goods out of small individual rooms at ground level. Wealthy patrons might, instead, be greeted by adorned versions of these shops with courtyards, fountains, and mosaics[2] designed to appeal to Rome's most exclusive clientele. In this way, commerce adapted to demographic needs, tailoring store design to the people of the city. As a result, the retail industry grew so robust that the streets of Ancient Rome were "...dominated more so by shops than by any other singular kind of building."[3]

In smaller towns or rural areas, temporary stalls might have been more appropriate for holding goods. Markets were no less important in these locations, however, with verbal exchanges uniting those who might rarely see one another otherwise. "A trip to market was a social occasion as well as an economic imperative."[4] Consequently, areas of commerce, regardless of size, became a place to exchange news and discover political developments.[5] By the 13th century, markets had become so popular that kings and other officials used them to communicate announcements, illustrating their powerful place of importance in the lives of citizens.[6]

Although location often influenced the merchandise and means of sale, there were other times in which trade directly shaped the community as well. For example, there are many instances throughout history when commerce arrived before a town was established and areas grew where the exchange of wares was most common, along trade routes, near ports, or in areas where unique products were available.[7] As travel to the area increased, other businesses, like restaurants and inns, became successful as well, and the community as a whole expanded. Research to this effect has "...transformed the

DOI: 10.4324/9781032616650-6

field of medieval economic history, directing scholarly attention away from demography and toward commercialization as the primary explanatory model for change in the period."[8] There is no doubt that commerce has been a powerful driver of change since ancient times.

Today, symbiotic relationships between community influences and the design of retail establishments remain. Economic, political, cultural, and social factors, as well as technological sources, continue to be responsible for these changes. As agrarian societies became industrialized, open-air markets, agoras, and bazaars gave way to multi-level department stores, strip malls, and indoor shopping malls, which, most recently, have given way to outlet malls, pop-up shops, and lifestyle centers. Modern society continues to impact the design of retail spaces; conversely, commerce persists in impacting the identity of communities.

A major issue, however, is that in the past, consumers were often limited by location for merchandise, with local resources as the only competition for similar products. Until only recently, physical stores were the primary method to locate and purchase goods, with very little buying completed through the mail.[9] This led to strong and unified shopping districts, maintaining a centralized message in keeping with the community's distinctive identity. With the rise of online shopping however,

> …more consumers are purchasing items via the internet and retailers are focusing much of their efforts towards growing the online extensions of their businesses. In America alone, virtual marketplaces are estimated to make between $150–200 billion annually and consumers are purchasing online at a higher rate than ever before.[10]

This leads to more empty store fronts on both Main Street and in the shopping malls, as retail establishments struggle to find a balance between cyber sales and in-store experiences for consumers. Ideally, brands maintain both experiences for shoppers, but they often struggle to determine what will draw in patrons to brick-and-mortar stores when products are so readily accessible online. Location plays an integral role in the physical changes that are necessary for success, but all too often businesses do not consider the positive attributes that the neighborhood can bring when designing their stores. Success occurs when shops value the potential connection to the greater community and the sense of place that is created in doing so, capitalizing on the network of those with common values and interests and the feeling of belonging that comes with that connection.

The Problem

To examine these issues in greater detail, a ten-week hypothetical design problem was presented to junior-level interior design studios at Thomas Jefferson University in the fall terms of 2020 and 2021. Thirty students, 29 females and 1 male, ranging in age from 20 to 25 years old, with most on the younger

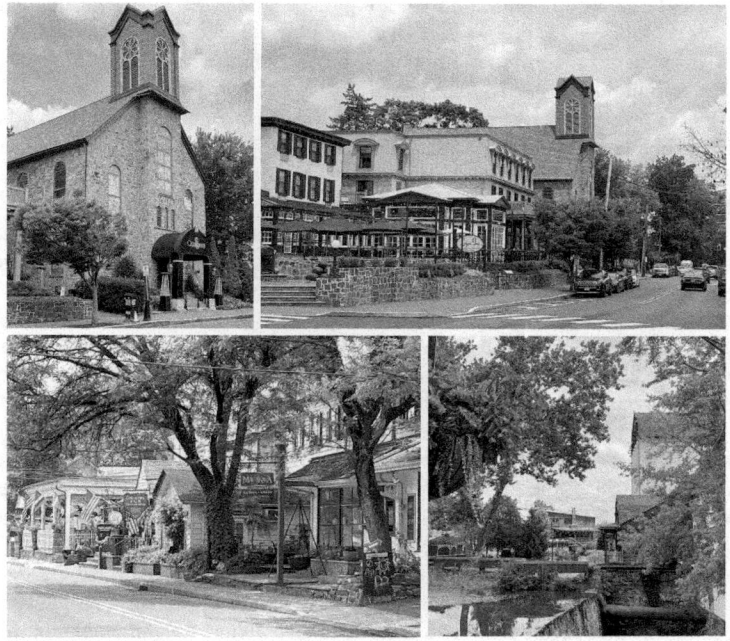

Figure 6.1 Church & General New Hope Main Street, images by Lisa Phillips.

end of this spectrum, comprised the two groups. The project was located in the small town of New Hope, PA, situated halfway between Philadelphia and New York City. For both years, an adaptive reuse site was utilized: a former small church, with the opportunity for three potential levels, on Main Street in the center of New Hope's commercial district (Figure 6.1). The large program of approximately 6,000 sf included a sales area, a manager's office, a break room, support areas, and a community space, and it required a distinctive retail experience, not a franchise or chain store, trying to satisfy all tastes.

The type of product focus for the new store varied from student to student, based on research conducted during the project. Research shows that merchandise selection for a retail store is a key decision in the business planning stages. The core values of a community, the conveniences and services it provides, the types and number of people it brings to its streets as potential shoppers, and a lack of competing stores in the area all need to be evaluated when considering if product sales will be successful in the town.[11] Assessing whether a store's brand and expected target audience resonate with the local identity is important for predicting whether or not the store can develop a successful long-term relationship with the community.

With this information in mind, the guiding principles for the assignment were as follows: (a) build a cohesive brand for the store, making sure that it aligns with the goals of the community and of potential consumers; (b) engage the community in brand-reinforcing spaces for consumers to gather; and (c) create an immersive retail experience for consumers that strengthens the brand and lengthens dwell time. Although the program was large for a typical retail store, students were asked to view the location as a brand defining experience, more like a flagship store for their brand, rather than a boutique shop.

To begin their research, students took into consideration the demographics of both the local area and current visitors to New Hope. The designers were required to interview members of the community to determine the types of retail establishments that were currently in the town and those that were not present at this time but that might be welcomed in the area. They also conducted a site study, analyzing both vehicular and pedestrian traffic at the site, sun and wind information, and sensory opportunities and obstacles.

Once a product focus was determined, branding was discussed, and each student developed an overall identity, including colors, materials, a logo, and a typography, for their retail establishment. The demographics of their target market within the community was considered as they created this brand. The next step was to conduct an extensive precedent study to learn about the optimal retail design principles for each stores' particular products. Two studies could be selected from magazines or books, while the third was a visited case study. The precedents examined entry sequence, fixtures, lighting conditions, colors and materials, spaces to build community, brand building within the space, and wayfinding methods in each store.

In addition to this research, New Hope's past was investigated for clues about how the proposed stores could connect to both the historical and modern heritage of the small riverside town. Although originally settled by Native American tribes many centuries prior, the town was not established by English settlers until the early 18th century. At that time, New Hope quickly became recognized as an important stop along the Delaware River due to its location halfway between New York City and Philadelphia. As such, it played a vital role in the preparation of several Revolutionary War battles.[12] During this time, New Hope was known more for its industry than its commerce, with large mills utilizing the local waterways to move products to market.[13] Meanwhile, its location, adjacent to the river and bucolic surrounding countryside, made it popular with painters, who eventually formed a school nearby.[14] Over time, the town became better known for its artisans and artists than its industry, and it remains known this way today.

Because of its rising property values, the result of being situated within a commutable distance to two major metropolitan cities, more artists presently visit New Hope than reside in the area. According to 2019 Census data, the town's population consists of 2,513 people. The median house value in the area is $589,700, far above the national average of $374,900. The majority of residents (89%) identify as Caucasian.[15]

Although there is not much diversity among New Hope's residents, a rich variety of tourists visit the town annually. Artists are joined by bohemians, alternative types, and motorcycle bikers. The stores are diverse as well, with crystal shops, smoke shops, psychics, and tattoo parlors alongside ice cream stores, bookshops, and artisanal markets. The town has largely resisted most outside corporate influences, except for a Starbucks and a Dunkin Donuts.

Students considered all these factors when designing their new retail establishment for New Hope. How would their decisions compliment the current community fabric? Would they connect to its industrial past or current artistic/alternative vibe; or might they consider what New Hope is missing and bring something new to the town? How might their retail design not only be influenced by, but also help to forge, the continually evolving identity of New Hope?

Research and Analysis

There is much evidence to suggest that while some brick-and-mortar retail stores may be struggling, if certain factors are taken into consideration, they cannot only survive, but they can thrive. Most research in current retails trends recommends both internal and external community building.

New Hope's stores, like others throughout the country, have been deeply impacted by both online shopping and the COVID-19 pandemic.[16] With fewer people physically out in the community, retailers must carefully consider what will not only bring them in, but also what will keep them in longer. In a shift of shopping culture, today's consumers are demonstrating that they favor experience over availability of products alone. This method of retail design requires the consideration of many layers within the program that can be designed to maximize the consumers' immersion in the store and the brand.

The exterior of the retail establishment, for example, is the first layer of the design seen by the neighborhood. Therefore, the establishment's signage and visual merchandising, color choices and textures, and whether or not it appears inviting or imposing will all determine if consumers will connect with this new store in their shopping district or not. For this reason, the exterior should never be overlooked for its important strategic ability to convey the brand's identity to all from the street and sidewalk and for the power to weave a narrative and grant a positive first impression to all who walk by, likely determining if a potential consumer will cross the threshold or continue walking. If the right cord is struck and the threshold is breached, the landing area, the zone just inside the store, is the next opportunity to continue establishing the store's identity, whether through a logo, familiar colors, music, or an established image or form. As shoppers move through the store, additional branding elements can continually reinforce the desired experience to the customer.

Third Places

In a post-lockdown survey conducted by GlobalData, 79% of participants selected "social interactions" when asked what they have missed about not being able to visit physical shops.[17] The fact that social interactions are so valuable to consumers is not surprising, since this behavior parallels the act of shopping throughout history. "For retailers, there is an opportunity to re-engage consumers through exciting and novel experiences centered around our inherent need for in-person connection."[18] With the advent of e-commerce, physical locations are free of their primary obligation to sell goods. Instead, the historical role of shopping as a way to "...escape, discover and learn"[19] can be revived.

There are multiple ways to engage consumers and build these experiential social environs. One method that is currently gaining traction is to add third places to retail establishments. The term "third place" originated in the 1980s with American urban socialist Ray Oldenburg.[20] It expands on a theory of Sigmund Freud, who believed people only need two places to be happy: home and work. Oldenburg elaborated on this idea by adding a "third place" that is "...inclusively sociable, offering both the basis of community and celebration of it."[21] Oldenburg explained that these environments include a "... great variety of public places that host the regular, voluntary, informal, and happily anticipated gatherings of individuals."[22] In the retail realm, third places exist in addition to merchandise displays and might include spaces designed to eat or drink, take classes, or relax with common-minded consumers.

Beyond the obvious advantages to shoppers, there are also benefits for retail establishments that have third spaces. A study by Mark S. Rosenbaum, an Assistant Professor of Marketing at Northern Illinois University, shows that adding these areas can create a culture of brand loyalty with patrons who not only stay longer, but also want to return more often.[23] His work noted three distinct categories of consumers: those who see a "place-as-practical"; those who view a "place-as-gathering"; and, those who experience a "place-as-home." In his study of a restaurant as a third place, he notes that some consumers visited primarily to satisfy the basic need to eat, while others came looking to socialize and others still to belong. In his analysis, he found loyalty to the establishment increased with each level of attachment, with those who saw it as a place of consumption being the least loyal and those who saw it as a second home being the most loyal.[24]

Even though a third place may be added to a retail environment, the design is only one of several elements that lead to the success of such spaces. Regardless of the type of activity chosen, the store will need to clearly communicate that the activities within are supported and welcomed in their store. An example of this can be seen in many bookstores that include cafes, where staff behavior does not discourage guests from borrowing and perusing books while they eat or drink. Additionally, there is no pressure for table turnover or sales. Third places are not provided as a means to promote immediate consumption; rather, they focus on fostering community and long-term brand loyalty.

In order to find the most appropriate types of third places to include, retail establishments must connect to a location's identity and examine the characteristics of consumers in the area. In a town like New Hope, this might include tapping into the existing artist demographic. Third places can also find inspiration in the store brand's merchandise and messaging to further communicate the business' guiding principles. Examples might include providing a cooking kitchen in a store that promotes healthy lifestyles or including a do-it-yourself beauty treatment area in a sustainable personal care shop. Ideally, connecting to both the community and brand will help to achieve ideal results.

Brand Engagement and Immersion

Retailers seeking to establish "…a sense of community are implementing environments that support immersive community interactions. It's not merely about the product, but about using unique fixtures and storytelling pieces to contextualize products in a relatable lifestyle."[25] Everything from a store's music to the colors, font selections, materials, and architecture reinforce the brand and the community that is built by that brand.

A retail establishment only grows a community by building familiarity with consumers by connecting to them and showing similarities to their core principles, their behaviors, and what they stand for. Doing this takes time, so a primary goal of modern stores is to increase the dwell time in any way possible, taking multiple opportunities to reinforce the brand by providing activities where the client can actively engage in meaningful interactions, many of which are not available online. Since they are in person, the chances of connecting to other consumers in the store will be higher. For many, simply interacting with physical products is enough of a draw. When that is not enough, stores are doubling down on a multitude of ways to interact, including in-store customization of their products. Although there are some customization services available online, the ability to have staff support is an added comfort, especially when these amenities are expensive. Such activities are often enjoyable in groups as well, which can increase the likelihood of multiple shoppers with a singular purpose.

Technology can provide many additional opportunities to delight and entertain in-store. Augmented reality, for example, can use a personal device, like a mobile phone or tablet, to add computer-generated layers over images of live objects in real time. It is increasingly used in retail environments to add additional information about products or to allow virtual testing of them. In addition, virtual reality headsets allow visitors to become fully immersed in games and product personalization. The use of artificial intelligence, holograms, and robots are also becoming more popular, as are interactive product displays and mirrors. The latter also allow virtual testing of merchandise. Interactive quizzes or games, used for entertainment, education, or product information, are often found in many modern brick-and-mortar retail establishments as well.

Lastly, it is vital to consider the power of social media culture and how stores appeal to consumers through sites like Instagram. In 2021, Instagram had 1.21 billion monthly active users, but it is predicted that this number will be closer to 1.44 billion by 2025, accounting for 31.2% of all internet users in the world.[26] These new consumers are seeking "…unique experiences … (and are) drawn to participatory moments. They want to be able to document their narratives on social media, but (they) also just crave things that are centered around connection, belonging, and status."[27] In response, many retail locations are not only allowing photos to be taken in their stores, but they are actually providing specific zones that are created for this purpose – Instagram areas.

These locations are not purely one-sided in their purpose, however. The retail establishment benefits greatly from their creation as well. When clients take photos with their friends and tag their location, it doesn't just fill their social media feed; it also provides exposure to the local business in the form of free advertising. This brings more clients to the store and also to the town. If the store is in keeping with the community brand, it is likely that other shops in the area will also benefit from additional visitors, as will local restaurants and other service industries. Building a strong online following can have considerable implications for the overall community and its continual growth.

Methods

After conducting this initial research and determining a merchandise focus and social strategy for their project, students began the design process in earnest. Students used various forms of media throughout their explorations, including physical models and computer-generated modeling, to develop their solutions. Mood boards and intensive furniture, finish, and accessory selections were reviewed, facilitating discussions of human behavior, ergonomics, light, color, and wayfinding. An intermediate critique was utilized to receive constructive feedback from professionals. Additionally, in the second year, virtual reality was used during the process portion of the project to provide a better sense of scale and materiality while creating the three-dimensional (3D) models. In many cases, the 3D immersions allowed the students to view and further resolve areas that had been neglected in the design or spaces that were either too cramped or open. A final critique was given at the end of ten weeks, requiring physical plots and materials, as well as a wood model of the completed project.

Solutions

A sampling of completed designs is featured below. In the first example, the retail establishment focused on ceramic pieces with neutral-colored, hand-thrown bowls, plates, mugs, and serving pieces as the main merchandise (Figure 6.2). This product type addressed the town's artistic personality well, although it had no direct competition on the current Main Street. A small coffee shop was included, featuring handmade mugs available for in-store purchase. On the second level, a large interactive and informational wall-mounted LED screen provided valuable historical information on ceramics to shoppers as they browsed. The most compelling social area, however, was featured on the third floor, which offered a clay throwing studio that provided both courses and pottery wheels to rent by the hour. The ability for groups to create together promotes a powerful and unique social connection, as has been seen in many other similar locations that offer artful services. Moreover, the experience is one that participants would likely share via social media.

Another student's design focused on high-end water-resistant products – a sensible consideration given the nearby river and the multitude of related sports that occur in the area. This store targeted the local wealthy residents of New Hope as clientele, an unusual choice among the students.

The design included a substantial waterproof testing exhibit that was three stories in height and allowed consumers to view pieces of rainwear being subjected to the elements and to witness their performance over time (Figure 6.2). This sculpture included technology, art, and wayfinding in the design. Other elements of technology were featured throughout the store to reinforce the brand. An in-store app allowed customers to link up to virtual reality mirrors that were located at multiple locations throughout the design, allowing them to try on merchandise virtually. Alongside designer rain jackets, rainboots, and umbrellas, several intimate gathering spaces with fireplaces for community use were tucked into the multi-floor design. These areas were not created for a specific purpose; instead, they were intended to provide informal gathering opportunities for the public. The arrangement and materials of the furniture encouraged socialization, and the various sizes throughout the store supported numerous types of gatherings, from large to small. The message that this store was a destination for the wider community to escape from the elements was evident not only through its merchandise but also its third places.

An unusual solution occurred when a student chose to look at a traditional product in a new way. In the modern world, photography is often relegated to mobile methods, but this individual created a remarkable camera store that

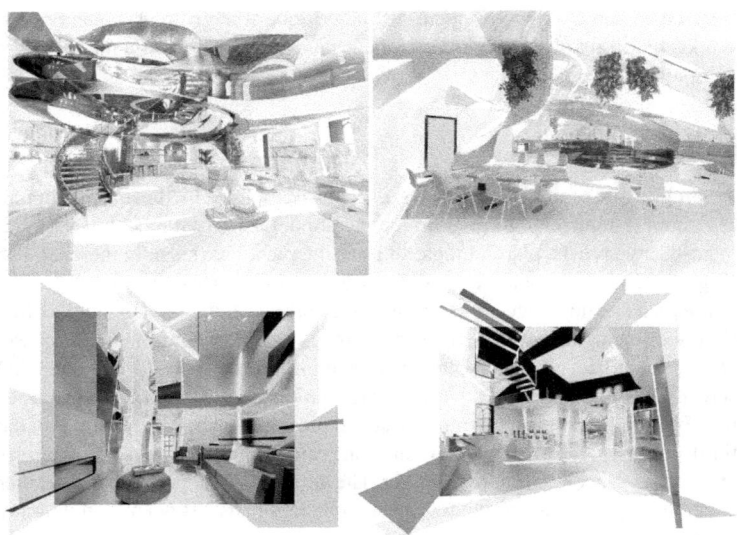

Figure 6.2 Above: Ceramic shop designed by TJU student, Ashley Hurst, below: Water-resistant retail store designed by TJU student, Madeleine Tickner.

was worth visiting in person (Figure 6.3). Appealing to the artistic nature of New Hope, she sold traditional products and provided a conventional dark room but also included modern photography equipment for mobile devices. The student's design offered photography classes, with the colorful backdrop of the store's branding well suited for patrons always on the lookout for their next Instagram or Tik-Tok post. There were also dynamic photo booths to interact with other shoppers in and ways to easily print images from digital devices. An interactive wall that provided techniques to change backgrounds and settings on cameras rounded out the design. With the ability to take photography classes out along the streets of New Hope, this store's impact on the local community promised to be especially effective.

At times, the suggested store did have competition in town but the design was so unique that it would still be able to draw in its own demographic. That was the case when a student suggested a sweets store that would focus on making the hands-on experience enjoyable for both children and adults (Figure 6.3). The store featured a candy-making station, where shoppers could take classes together. The student also included a "design your own label" station on the third floor, where individuals or groups could gather to customize creations or purchases. The most exciting element, however, was a creative robot arm she designed to pick up the desired sweets and drop them into a container to be procured by the customer. During the pandemic, especially,

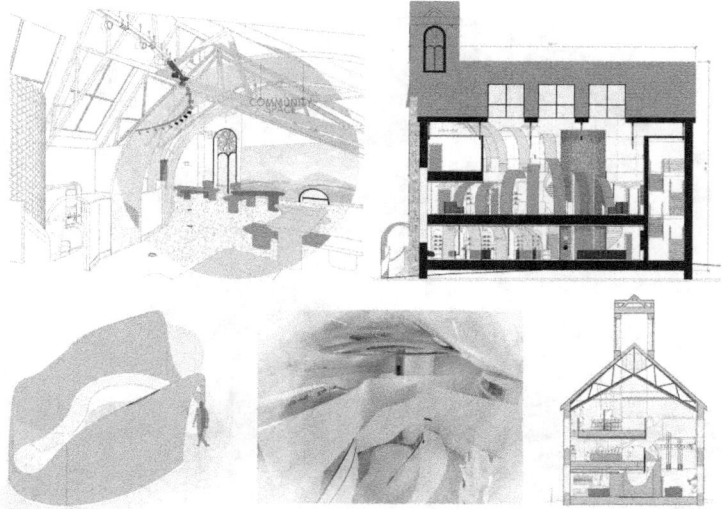

Figure 6.3 Above: Photography Store designed by TJU student, Mallory Katen; below: Ice cream and sweet shop designed by TJU student, Caylin Munn.

this would prevent cross contamination of the candy. It is not difficult to imagine that this feature would become popular with children and would likely become part of the identity of the store and New Hope alike.

Two students chose to focus their retail establishments on areas of expansion rather than the current demographics of New Hope. The first noted that there was a strong female emphasis in many of the stores in town and that few establishments addressed male consumers. Therefore, she designed a clothing and accessory store with men in mind; her design balanced rough textures with sleek, high-end customization technology (Figure 6.4). The primary community space was on the third floor: a cigar bar that served dark alcohols, including bourbons, whiskies, rums, and beer. Other areas that reinforced her store's brand, however, were a touch pad customization area and an augmented reality mirror, where viewers could see the customized items on themselves before purchasing. This design proposal appealed deeply to the history of New Hope as a location of industry, a working man's town.

Another store that also recognized a demographic gap was one aimed at increasing the diversity of New Hope, specifically expanding brown and black representation in the area by providing a store to purchase high-end sneakers and streetwear (Figure 6.4). The student featured customization screens for the sneakers and clothing items that were only available in-store. Larger-than-life, interactive games were also available throughout the space to encourage interaction with friends or fellow consumers. The bright colors

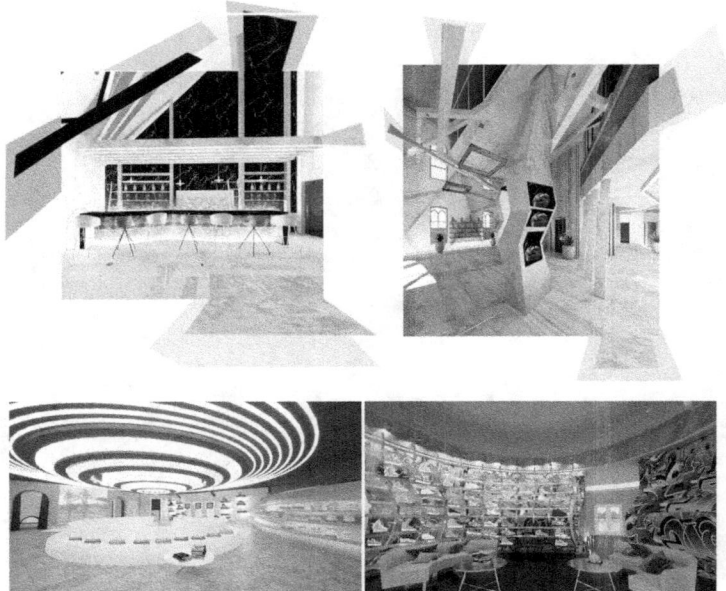

Figure 6.4　Above: Men's clothing and accessory store designed by TJU student, Victoria Sioutis; below: Sneaker and streetwear retail store designed by TJU student, Maylene Reyes.

and graffiti-inspired graphic walls created a lively and welcoming design that would generate vivid backgrounds for customers' social media posts.

Finally, one additional store, which sold jeans as its primary merchandise, deserves mentioning. This space featured jeans throughout history and allowed buyers to purchase styles from across the decades in addition to contemporary trends (Figure 6.5). The community space in this store allowed users to customize their purchases with tailoring and to personalize distressing and design patches. With the continued popularity of jeans, coupled with the complexity of purchasing them online, this retail typology would have the potential for significant foot traffic from a wide demographic in New Hope.

Assessment

The variety and complexity of both the merchandise selections and the intended target consumers showed considerable diversity throughout the course of the two semesters the project has been assigned. The solutions have exhibited thoughtful and informed research and concern for the continual

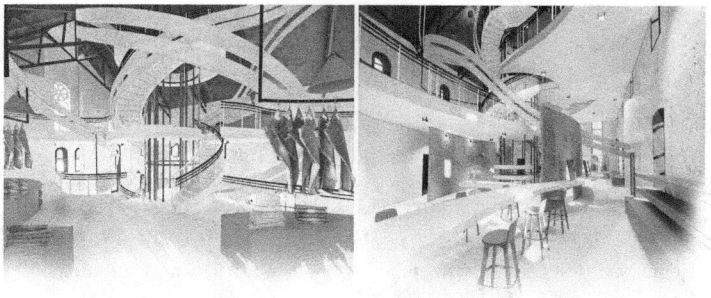

Figure 6.5 Jean shop designed by TJU student, Kaylie Siwy.

connection to the New Hope community, likely fostered by the site visits and interviews with residents, visitors, and shop owners.

Students often reflect that this project is impactful to them on multiple levels. They appreciate the historic location in the town of New Hope and the ability to select a product focus for the store that is unique to each of them. In addition to the community connection providing a distinctive goal that they find both challenging and fulfilling, the students are also able to deeply explore many aspects of interior design throughout this project. As they build their store's brand identity, ideas about color, light quality, and textures weave into the narrative, continually strengthening the sensory experience for the consumer. Wayfinding further extends the brand. One student, Summer Long, discussed the subject of wayfinding as a source of personal growth in her own project. She noted that "… providing occupants of a space with a form of wayfinding other than through the use of signage is very beneficial and can make the design a lot more manoeuvrable and give the design potential to be a lot more interactive as well." Her design for a game store in the town featured merchandise from across the decades, including classic versions and more recent beloved games as well. The included wayfinding featured colors to signify departments within her store, with floors changing hues that could be viewed through an open atrium space.

Tori Gerardi, another interior design student who participated in the fall 2021 semester's project, felt that the nature of the assignment helped her to "…. get to know the community well (and that) helped in making decisions during the process and allowed (her) to feel more passionate for the project." Tori's client and merchandise were deeply inspired by her visit to and research on New Hope, where she learned that there were many families with teenagers both in the area and arriving as shoppers. Her skateboard retail space with interior areas for skating in-store focused on a demographic that was underrepresented within the community. She felt that giving teens in the region a place to call their own within the store would benefit not just her brand but also the neighborhood overall. Since many of the current New Hope stores were currently aimed at adults, bored teens could linger and find their "people" within her retail establishment.

The final design critique for the project was attended by design professionals, several of whom had direct experience in retail design. They agreed that the work connected community and retail in a unique manner and that the project had many elements that, although hypothetical, required students to interact with the site and the neighborhood in a way that strengthened the final results.

Quantifiable assessment of the project was conducted through a rubric scored by the instructor. The criteria that were used to determine the success of the outcomes were as follows: "Focus of store was justified for location" and "Design engaged community." The target set for each of the criteria was that at least 85% of the class should score in the average category (three on a scale from one to five) or higher. For the "Focus of store was justified for location" category, 100% of the students scored average or better, and for the "Design engaged community" category, over 96% of the students scored an average or better score on the rubric; thus, the classes met the target set in both cases. In the few projects that were average, third places were included, but they were generic rather than specific to the store's merchandise or the community's identity.

Reflecting on the project as a professor, I believe that this assignment is easily transferable on many levels. It can be replicated in another design studio in a different city, state, or county, as long as research into the demographic conditions and existing retail establishments is conducted. It is also transferable by the students, as the knowledge they have obtained in the project can be applicable to future courses and tasks. Understanding informed evidence-based design is a skill that will always stay relevant, as students received excellent experience conducting interviews, neighborhood analyses, and case study investigations during this project.

There are ways that I might modify the project moving forward or suggestions I might make to others seeking to create similar assignments. I believe that the link to the community was the strongest aspect of this project. One idea I might include in the future is to have students maintain a connection with those whom they interview so that they can receive additional input throughout the process. This would also create a benefit for the neighborhood residents and shop keepers as well, as this project currently offers them no particular advantages. An additional idea, building on one of the final stores I discussed, would address minority communities. Through my research I have found evidence connecting the growth of retail establishments to the building of stronger communities.[28] Supporters of this research note that the more stores there are in neighborhoods, the more they raise tax revenues, create jobs, and make "… more attractive places for working families and individuals to live."[29] Rather than base the project in an affluent neighborhood, another option would be to utilize a standard pre-engineered building and have students locate a site in a marginalized neighborhood of their choosing. In this way, they would be able to further personalize the project, which I find increases student motivation and their individual connection to the assignment. There may also be ways to work with other designers at our university and create real pop-up shops in communities. A real-world client and project installation would be ideal but may be complicated, as we would need to work with non-profit organizations for pro-bono services.

Conclusions

Commerce and the local community share a symbiotic relationship. The growth of one affects the other, and this relationship continually changes the evolving narrative of a place. There is growing evidence that there are a multitude of ways to connect consumers to both the brand of the retail establishment and, in turn, the identity of the neighborhood. Formalized areas of socialization and immersive brand building are but a few of the newest methods available to do this. These mirror the kinds of social activities that have paralleled commerce throughout history. Careful examination of a location by investigating demographics, history, and other factors can help to identify the types of activities that are appropriate for a town's retail spaces and assist in designing third places and other interactive activities that will appeal to patrons.

The interior design students in this study provided wide-ranging solutions, but a majority met the project's goals of considering both the historic and current identities of New Hope in their designs. The choices for merchandise and social concepts were closely tied to the town's narrative, and, although hypothetical in nature, their solutions reveal much about the continual evolution and relationship of commerce and community.

Notes

1 Ian Johnston, "How the Most Progressive Retailers Are Driving Positive Impact in Society," *Quinine,* accessed July 22, 2022, https://quininedesign.com/perspectives/retail-and-society.
2 Alexander Gorlin, "Alexander Gorlin Architects," The Shops of Ancient Rome - Interior Design, accessed July 22, 2022, https://gorlinarchitects.com/writings/interior-design-one.
3 Steven J. R. Ellis, *The Roman Retail Revolution: The Socio-Economic World of the Taberna* (Oxford: Oxford University Press, 2018), 4.
4 James Masschaele, "The Public Space of the Marketplace in Medieval England," *Speculum* 77, no. 2 (2002): 383–421, https://doi.org/10.2307/3301326.

5 Johnston, "How the Most Progressive Retailers Are Driving Positive Impact in Society."

6 Masschaele, "The Public Space of the Marketplace in Medieval England," 390.

7 M. P. Charlesworth, *Trade-Routes and Commerce of the Roman Empire* (Cambridge: Cambridge University Press, 2016).

8 Masschaele, 383.

9 "Internet's Impact on Retailers in the Age of Growing Marketplaces," impacX, May 18, 2021, https://impacx.io/blog/internet-affects-retailers/.

10 "Internet's Impact on Retailers in the Age of Growing Marketplaces."

11 Edward, M. Mazze, "Identifying the Key Factors in Retail Store Location." *Journal of Small Business Management* (Pre-1986), Suppl. Winter 10 (01, 1972): 17. https://www.proquest.com/scholarly-journals/identifying-key-factors-retail-store-location/docview/210750278/se-2.

12 "History of New Hope: New Hope Borough, PA," History of New Hope | New Hope Borough, PA, accessed July 22, 2022, https://www.newhopeborough.org/209/History-of-New-Hope.

13 "History - Historic New Hope, Pennsylvania," Greater New Hope Chamber of Commerce, accessed July 22, 2022, https://www.visitnewhope.com/history/.

14 "History of New Hope" and "History - Historic New Hope, Pennsylvania."

15 "New Hope, PA," Data USA, accessed July 24, 2022, https://datausa.io/profile/geo/new-hope-pa#:~:text=In%202019%2C%20New%20Hope%2C%20PA,%2489%2C861%2C%20a%203.11%25%20increase.

16 "Natural Food Merchandiser. Reimagine Retail: COVID-19 Will Keep Changing How Consumers Shop," New Hope Network, accessed July 24, 2022, https://www.newhope.com/retail-and-distribution/reimagine-retail-covid-19-will-keep-changing-how-consumers-shop.

17 "Multichannel Retail and COVID-19 Report: Consumer and Retailer Behavior during Pandemic Demonstrate Online and Physical Sales Channels Form a Highly Competitive Single Retail Market According to Latest Research by GlobalData," *GlobalData*, September 15, 2020, accessed July 22, 2022, https://www.globaldata.com/multichannel-retail-covid-19-report-consumer-retailer-behavior-pandemic-demonstrate-online-physical-sales-channels-form-highly-competitive-single-retail-market-according-lates/.

18 Michael Gatti, "How Social Interactions Will Drive Retail Forward," *Gensler*, November 22, 2021, accessed July 22, 2022, https://www.gensler.com/blog/how-social-interactions-will-drive-retail-forward.

19 Johnston.

20 Ray Oldenburg, *The Great Good Place: Cafés, Coffee Shops, Bookstores, Bars, Hair Salons, and Other Hangouts at the Heart of a Community* (Philadelphia, PA: Da Capo Press, 2005).

21 Oldenburg, *The Great Good Place*, 14.

22 Oldenburg, 16.

23 Mark S. Rosenbaum, "Exploring the Social Supportive Role of Third Places in Consumers' Lives," *Journal of Service Research* 9, no. 1 (2006): 59–72, https://doi.org/10.1177/1094670506289530.

24 Rosenbaum, "Exploring the Social Supportive Role of Third Places in Consumers' Lives," 61–62.

25 Patrick Flood, "Retail Spaces That Build Community," Retail Design - Pop-up Shops - Shop-in-Shop - Branded Experience, August 9, 2019, accessed February 19, 2023, https://www.q20lab.com/retail-spaces-that-build-community.

26 S. Dixon, "Instagram Users Worldwide 2025," Statista, May 23, 2022, accessed February 19, 2023, https://www.statista.com/statistics/183585/instagram-number-of-global-users/#:~:text=In%202021%2C%20there%20were%201.21,percent%20of%20global%20internet%20users.

27 Digital Main Street, "Instagram Continues to Influence Design in Retail Environments and Public Spaces," Digital Main Street, March 1, 2019, accessed February 19, 2023, https://digitalmainstreet.ca/instagram-is-changing-our-public-spaces/.

28 Rick Jacobus and Karen Chapple, "What Difference Can a Few Stores Make Retail and Neighborhood ...," What difference can a few stores make? Retail and neighborhood revitalization (Center for Community Innovation, June 2010), accessed February 19, 2023, https://communityinnovation.berkeley.edu/sites/default/files/what_difference_can_a_few_stores_make_retail_and_neighborhood_revitalization.pdf?width=1200&height=800&iframe=true.

29 Jacobus and Chapple, "What Difference Can a Few Stores Make?"

References

Charlesworth, M. P. *Trade-Routes and Commerce of the Roman Empire*. Cambridge: Cambridge University Press, 2016.

Digital Main Street. "Instagram Continues to Influence Design in Retail Environments and Public Spaces." Digital Main Street, March 1, 2019. Accessed February 19, 2023. https://digitalmainstreet.ca/instagram-is-changing-our-public-spaces/.

Dixon, S. "Instagram Users Worldwide 2025." Statista, May 23, 2022. Accessed February 19, 2023. https://www.statista.com/statistics/183585/instagram-number-of-global-users/#:~:text=In%202021%2C%20there%20were%201.21,percent%20of%20global%20internet%20user.

Ellis, Steven J. R. *The Roman Retail Revolution: The Socio-Economic World of the Taberna*. Oxford: Oxford University Press, 2018.

Flood, Patrick. "Retail Spaces That Build Community." Retail Design - Pop-up Shops - Shop-in-Shop - Branded Experience, August 9, 2019. Accessed February 19, 2023. https://www.q20lab.com/retail-spaces-that-build-community.

Gatti, Michael. "How Social Interactions Will Drive Retail Forward." *Gensler*, November 22, 2021. Accessed July 22 2022. https://www.gensler.com/blog/how-social-interactions-will-drive-retail-forward.

Gorlin, Alexander. "Alexander Gorlin Architects." The Shops of Ancient Rome - Interior Design. Accessed July 22, 2022. https://gorlinarchitects.com/writings/interior-design-one.

"History - Historic New Hope, Pennsylvania." Greater New Hope Chamber of Commerce. Accessed July 22, 2022. https://www.visitnewhope.com/history/.

"History of New Hope: New Hope Borough, PA." History of New Hope | New Hope Borough, PA. Accessed July 22, 2022. https://www.newhopeborough.org/209/History-of-New-Hope.

"Internet's Impact on Retailers in the Age of Growing Marketplaces." impacX, May 18, 2021. https://impacx.io/blog/internet-affects-retailers/.

Jacobus, Rick and Karen Chapple. "What Difference Can a Few Stores Make Retail and Neighborhood ..." What difference can a few stores make? Retail and neighborhood revitalization. Center for Community Innovation, June 2010. Accessed February 19, 2023. https://communityinnovation.berkeley.edu/sites/default/files/what_difference_can_a_few_stores_make_retail_and_neighborhood_revitalization.pdf?width=1200&height=800&iframe=true.

Johnston, Ian. "How the Most Progressive Retailers Are Driving Positive Impact in Society." *Quinine*. Accessed July 22, 2022. https://quininedesign.com/perspectives/retail-and-society.

Masschaele, James. "The Public Space of the Marketplace in Medieval England." *Speculum* 77, no. 2 (April 2002): 383–421. https://doi.org/10.2307/3301326.

Mazze, Edward M. "Identifying the Key Factors in Retail Store Location." *Journal of Small Business Management* (Pre-1986), Suppl. Winter 10 (01, 1972): 17. https://www.proquest.com/scholarly-journals/identifying-key-factors-retail-store-location/docview/210750278/se-2.

"Multichannel Retail and COVID-19 Report: Consumer and Retailer Behavior during Pandemic Demonstrate Online and Physical Sales Channels Form a Highly Competitive Single Retail Market According to Latest Research by GlobalData." GlobalData, September 15, 2020. Accessed July 22, 2022. https://www.globaldata.com/multichannel-retail-covid-19-report-consumer-retailer-behavior-pandemic-demonstrate-online-physical-sales-channels-form-highly-competitive-single-retail-market-according-lates/.

"Natural Food Merchandiser. Reimagine Retail: COVID-19 Will Keep Changing How Consumers Shop." New Hope Network. Accessed July 24, 2022. https://www.newhope.com/retail-and-distribution/reimagine-retail-covid-19-will-keep-changing-how-consumers-shop.

"New Hope, PA." Data USA. Accessed July 22, 2022. https://datausa.io/profile/geo/new-hope-pa#:~:text=In%202019%2C%20New%20Hope%2C%20PA,%2489%2C861%2C%20a%203.11%25%20increase.

Oldenburg, Ray. *The Great Good Place: Cafés, Coffee Shops, Bookstores, Bars, Hair Salons, and Other Hangouts at the Heart of a Community*. Philadelphia, PA: Da Capo Press, 2005.

Rosenbaum, Mark S. "Exploring the Social Supportive Role of Third Places in Consumers' Lives." *Journal of Service Research* 9, no. 1 (2006): 59–72. https://doi.org/10.1177/1094670506289530.

7 Conclusion

Kirsty Macari

Those within this book and beyond recognise that there is a role for art and design education in encouraging, acknowledging and promoting cultural awareness and intercultural discourse through the practice of learning. The act of making can encourage a sense of belonging beyond that which we would normally be associated with. It creates an environment with which to expand knowledge.

It could be considered that those driving the changes are our creative learners and alumni such as those who formed Decolonise Architecture[1] or educators and students which developed Bartlett Alternative.[2] Collectives which house a growing archive or work in their laboratory are providing alternative narratives and reconceptualised perspectives in relation to the built environment that encourage interdisciplinarty. It is those who will go both now and beyond us through education that will challenge current discourse. Learners now come with a confidence to question and a willingness to enquire both of themselves and of others. Educators should embrace opportunities to apply this regularly and rigorously whether through engaged teaching, experiential learning, socially orientated pedagogy or any other named definition that can create an environment for cultural discourse and enhance understanding.

As discussed in Chapter 2, there is a need to recognise the contribution that different cultures make to the history of art and design and also facilitate this as part of the learning process within an institutions curriculum and ensure a transformation beyond the attempts to date. There is much work to be done by both institutions and the academics within them to ensure that the space is created to allow student exploration.

If we think about what the future texts will look like, we are already seeing this being shaped by the "alternatives" with a growing database and open invite to contribute both literature and work that will shape collective curriculums both now and in the future. However, it is not only them and Chapter 2 clearly evidences the need for educators to understand and be informed by their own lived experience. It encourages acknowledgement of bias and the influence it has on how one may view culture. This is also linked to the need to understand our values as set out in Chapter 4.

DOI: 10.4324/9781032616650-7

Art and design can encourage both social activism and storytelling through mediums of education exploration and experiential learning beyond the classroom with communities and as critically and culturally conscious creators of tomorrow. In Chapter 3, the use of product outputs, including jewellery and furniture, a longer-term approach to students immersing themselves in socio-cultural issues and tackling wicked questions, is evident. It allowed students to explore South and West African, traditional Japanese material culture and the Shakers as a small example of the outputs gathered over 12 years of delivery. It is hoped that these products can continue to facilitate social activism.

The need for storytelling and the importance of having a medium for exploration are key as further highlighted in Chapter 5 with the visit to Yame, Japan. The use of film allowed students from both the UK and Japan to collaborate in the investigation of the heritage of Yame, making comparisons and growing knowledge of past, present and future visitors of the city. Embedding field trips within the curriculum and framing is one way in which to do this but may not be an option open to all. A challenge towards the future is ensuring there is no disadvantage when field trips may not be an option.

Chapter 6 clearly identifies the symbiotic relationships that can occur either within the education experience or within the environment with which they are based. These relationships, shown within the chapter linking community and commerce, are long established and with clear evidence of how retail, branding and neighbourhoods are all relative in understanding the social experiences of a place.

Each chapter has a series of transferable approaches that can be delivered within a different city or country and by any institution. The product outputs and the links to identity of place and consumerism are evident. These examples, considering cultural and social concerns across several regions of the world, are drawn together in a collective ambition in considering how we better educate students around the issues of cultural awareness. Each example provokes thoughts, ideas and conversations about how we engage.

How do we ensure we remain culturally engaged? As evidenced in the previous chapters, the ability to embed experiential learning ensures ways in which we can embrace building cultural knowledge, driven by the foundations of art and design disciplines as a means of enquiry. These positions are enhanced by Lalonde,[3] who emphasises relationship building and cultural protocols as necessary in forming the partnerships required to take any project or product from start to finish. In doing so ensuring that ongoing dialogue avoids issues of misrecognition or indeed nonrecognition of cultural awareness and minimising the risk of unintended cultural appropriation.

Opportunities to encourage mentorship between individuals can provide spaces for constructive discussion and feedback opportunities. The action point by Decolonise Architecture to create anonymous post-review feedback systems used to highlight issues within the design review process could be adopted within the wider studio review across art and design to highlight further decolonising curriculum opportunities. Ultimately facilitating mutual understanding through authentic but also evocative exchanges should be enhanced. Perhaps this should also be done for the curriculums across different art and design-based programmes.

Social media and access to immediate content on a global scale will continue to grow but will come with the challenge of deciphering what is true. AI may become a tool to allow the analysis of artefacts, film, music and art, perhaps enhancing a global perspective beyond that of the traditional classroom. It can support efficient language translation of materials from or into multiple languages and can facilitate intercultural exchanges. As a tool, it may encourage exploration and reinterpretation of cultural elements as part of the creative process and future innovation of artistic expression. There will need to be careful consideration of the implications of bias and privacy as part of ethical concerns that may arise. It is unlikely to replace the value and experience gained from the physical experience of the case studies within this book.

If we consider back to Kolb's position of experiential learning as a "process whereby knowledge is created through the transformation of experience. Knowledge results from the combination of grasping and transforming experience."[4] This, alongside the different experiences offered within this book, allows us to see art and design as a platform by which, and through, a focus on process can expand the existing approaches to learning and teaching. Atkinson[5] describes it as a "creative force of transformation beyond the capture of representation, identity, established knowledge and established aesthetic parameters." He goes on to describe an "adventure of pedagogy"[6] in relation to art and design and the understanding that this can offer in approach and challenge of existing and well-established knowledge and practice where learners may more openly debate the curriculum's content or the methods for learning.

Each chapter is connected through the need to ensure that artist and designer students should be encouraged to immersive themselves in critical questioning of not just themselves but also the cultures that they are exploring. Through sensitive but clear enquiry and ongoing reflection, it is possible to enhance critical thinking framed through cultural awareness. Each chapter is an example of both critical consciousness and cultural competence that is driven by the student learning experience.

Notes

1 "Decolonise Architecture Alternative Reading List," Decolonise Architecture, accessed December 1, 2023, https://www.decolonisearchitecture.com/alternative-reading-list.
2 Bartlett Alternative, "About Us," accessed December 2, 2023, https://www.bartlettalternative.com/about-us/.
3 Dianne Lalonde, "Does Cultural Appropriation Cause Harm?" *Politics, Groups, and Identities* 9, no. 2 (2021), https://doi.org/10.1080/21565503.2019.1674160.

112   *Kirsty Macari*

4 David Kolb, *Experiential Learning: Experience as the Source of Learning and Development* (Hoboken, NJ: Prentice-Hall, 1984), 41.

5 Dennis Atkinson, "The Force of Art," in *Art, Disobedience, and Ethics. Education, Psychoanalysis, and Social Transformation* (Cham: Palgrave Macmillan, 2018), 156. https://doi.org/10.1007/978-3-319–62639-0_8.

6 Atkinson, "The Force of Art," 206.

References

Atkinson, Dennis. *Art, Disobedience, and Ethics, Education, Psychoanalysis, and Social Transformation*. Cham: Palgrave Macmillan, 2018. p. 156. DOI 10.1007/978-3-319-62639-0_8.

Bartlett Alternative. "About Us." Accessed December 2, 2023. https://www.bartlettalternative.com/about-us/.

Decolonise Architecture. "Decolonise Architecture Alternative Reading List." Accessed December 1, 2023. https://www.decolonisearchitecture.com/alternative-reading-list.

Lalonde, Dianne. "Does Cultural Appropriation Cause Harm?" *Politics, Groups, and Identities* 9, no. 2 (2021): 329–346. https://doi.org/10.1080/21565503.2019.1674160.

Kolb, David A. *Experiential Learning: Experience as the Source of Learning and Development*. New Jersey: Prentice-Hall, 1984.

Index

Note: *Italic* page numbers refer to figures and page numbers followed by "n" denote endnotes.

For Product Safety Concerns and Information please contact our EU
representative GPSR@taylorandfrancis.com
Taylor & Francis Verlag GmbH, Kaufingerstraße 24, 80331 München, Germany

www.ingramcontent.com/pod-product-compliance
Lightning Source LLC
Chambersburg PA
CBHW070234180526
45158CB00001BA/498